Riding the Wave

*Good luck as you
navigate your "river"!*

Judy Phillips

Riding the Wave
A journey of continuous improvement

by
Thomas Houlihan and Judy S. Phillips

San Antonio
2002

Copyright 2002 by The Andrews Group

All rights reserved, For permission to use material from this book for purposes other than review, address
The Andrews Group
405 Commons Walk Circle
Morrisville, NC 27560-7854

First Edition

A Watercress Press book
From *Geron & Associates*, San Antonio, Texas

Book design by Alice Geron
Graphics by Lenella Meister

Library of Congress Control Number 2002115638
ISBN 0-934955-52-2

Printed and bound in the United States of America

ACKNOWLEDGEMENTS

First and foremost, the authors wish to express sincere appreciation to Andrew Phillips for his work on this book. From story ideas, editing, blending of the authors' writing styles, to working as liaison with the publisher, he has been an extremely valuable contributor. A huge thanks to Andrew Phillips, a talented writer in his own right.

We also wish to thank the North Carolina Partnership for Excellence "family," including teachers, board members, state policy makers, and school system participants, for providing the impetus so necessary to turn theory into reality. The decade of the 1990's was a "golden age" in North Carolina's education system. Student achievement gains led the nation in literally every conceivable measure. *Riding the Wave* reflects part of the theory and practice behind these achievement gains, and the NCPE family deserves much appreciation and thanks.

Riding the Wave is a joint effort between the authors and the North Carolina Partnership for Excellence. NCPE is a 501(c)-3 non-profit organization serving the public schools of North Carolina. A portion of the proceeds from the sale of this book supports the work of NCPE. This joint venture has allowed all of us to share our belief in the power of High Performance to influence education improvement.

We also wish to acknowledge the many partners who comprise the Center for High Performance—a network of states and school systems across the nation who are supported by a grant from the Atlantic Philanthropic Service Company, Inc. Thanks to practitioners in Colorado, Indiana, South Carolina, Tennessee, Washington, and Washington, D.C.

Finally, we want to acknowledge Drew Houlihan, a second-grade teacher at A.B. Combs Elementary School in Raleigh, North Carolina. Drew has been a true inspiration in taking these ideas as a beginning teacher and demonstrating what can happen when theory and reality are meshed into one.

TO THE READER

Riding the Wave is a sequel to our first book, *CommonSense.com*, and as such is designed to take the reader into a deeper and hopefully greater understanding of the necessary factors of high performance in our education systems. The learners in this sequel are the same as in our first book, and just as you will hopefully learn more, so do our main players as they journey forward on their quest for continuous improvement.

We have very consciously chosen the "story form" of approach to sharing new information, for we have found that some of the most significant learning takes place when applying key concepts to a parable, story or other form of written expression. The success of *CommonSense.com* encouraged us to continue in this type of format. Reader after reader shared with us how easy it was to grasp the four "bytes" of information presented through the parable described in the book. If *Riding the Wave* is even half as successful as our first venture, then we will have succeeded in helping others further their knowledge and understanding of the concept of continuous improvement.

Tom and Judy

Thanks for continuing your journey.

CONTENTS

Foreword	....	viii
Prologue:	And In the Beginning...	1
One	A Challenge to Align	13
Two	A Dream Is Like a River	25
Three	Leadership	35
Four	Customer Aims	45
Five	Goals and Measures	59
Six	Information Systems	69
Seven	Key Work Processes	79
Eight	Human Resources	93
Nine	Results	103
Ten	A Time for Farewells	113
Epilogue	....	117
Life is a Mystery!	....	118

FOREWORD

Public education in our country continues to be the subject of intense scrutiny, debate, and controversy. As an example, think back to the recent 2000 presidential election — this seemingly excessive level of scrutiny has created both resentment and resistance among educators who work in our schools every day. Many educators are quite concerned that schools are the subject of constant debate, and resent on a deeply personal level the politicization of American education.

This type of reaction will neither improve nor solve the politics of the profession. Instead this scrutiny, criticism, and questioning are actually a challenge that all must take to heart and help to overcome. Customers have the right and responsibility to voice their thoughts, praise, and concern regarding public institutions, including schools and school systems. It is a healthy aspect of our democracy, and instead of being resentful, educators should turn this scrutiny into an agenda of continuous improvement.

The key to success is not to become frustrated with all the talk about education but to turn these negative thoughts into positive action. Most people learn far more from controversy than they do when everything seems to be all right. It becomes a matter of perspective, and action based on perspective must be positive, productive, and grounded in both theory and practical application of that theory.

So how do we begin this journey? First, educators must realize that change and improvement cannot be accomplished via the "silver bullet" mentality. Improvement is hard, hard work and takes commitment and perseverance. After all, if improvement *were* easy, it would have already been implemented.

Second, it is critical that the quest for improvement be based on reflection and professional expertise—not simply reactive behavior. Most educators go to work every day with an internal motivation to be the best they can be. The commitment is there, but often the internal drive is not matched with the knowledge and skills to make change and improvement. It is through thoughtful reflection and professional expertise that the needed skills will come to make change in education organizations.

And finally, keep in mind that maximizing an organization's performance is based on a systems approach. We just can't "fix" one program, practice, or department. To be ultimately successful, we must change the system.

To repeat a fundamental belief of the Chinese proverb, "The journey of a thousand miles begins with the first step." In other words, begin your journey by looking at yourself and reflecting on the teachings shared in this book.

Enjoy the journey!

Riding the Wave

Prologue

AND IN THE BEGINNING . . .

Welcome to Andrews School

As if looking down from the clouds into the building of a school, John, Mary, and Jerri could see a crowd of students sitting in the bleachers of a gym or multi-purpose room. Many adults were sitting with the students, and a group of people sat on a stage facing the students. In many ways this gathering looked like a school assembly of some sort, with a speaker's podium in the middle of the platform of guests.

As they watched, the three saw a man in a dark blue suit stand up to address the audience. He said, "On behalf of the entire state, I want to congratulate all of you at Andrews School for being recognized as an exemplary school for your outstanding accomplishments. As Governor of this state, it gives me great pleasure to present you with this plaque commemorating your exemplary status and to say that Andrews School is viewed as a 'school that can,' having demonstrated over the last ten years that student performance, employee morale, and leadership can be combined to produce outstanding results. You should be very proud of your accomplishments."

With that the audience burst into a round of applause, and students and teachers began to cheer and "high five" one another. The Governor continued, "Your designation as exemplary has been achieved by only a handful of schools in the state. Exemplary status means student performance is significantly above expectation levels and that employee and community involvement has been outstanding. While there are many schools with similar characteristics, in terms of size, student population, and demographics, you have shown the world that being average doesn't mean being just like everyone else. What a great accomplishment you have achieved. I think you would agree that if it can happen at Andrews School it can happen in any school in our state and nation."

The Governor then shook the hands of the people sitting on the platform, presented a plaque to an individual, and then took his seat. As this was happening the audience clapped and cheered once again.

Following the Governor, another adult stood up to address the crowd. With a sense of pride that was obvious to everyone in the room, this person said, "When I became principal of Andrews School ten years ago, I knew the philosophy I was bringing to our school was very different. First, I knew this school did not belong to me. Instead, it belongs to the students, faculty, and community. I knew that certain things had to happen differently if all of you were going to believe that this school was yours, not mine.

"I knew when we created the mission statement for our school that many of you thought it was a waste of time. But I knew the time we spent up front creating a shared mission statement was critical, because the emphasis of a driving mission for our school was the first step in transforming Andrews School into the best that we could be. And I really believe that ownership of our school has become a shared vision not only because of this award today, but because I know in my heart that you believe this is your school . . . our school, not mine or the Board of Education. Am I right?"

The audience erupted into "Yes, Yes, Yes" in response to the principal's question, clapping and cheering both the principal and themselves as the Governor and other officials sat watching in amazement.

As the noise level in the assembly quieted, the principal continued, "The second change I thought was important was to involve our employees, and I mean all employees, in the day-to-day decision-making of our school. While I have always maintained that certain responsibilities cannot be delegated, such as discipline and school safety, I have practiced the belief that many day-to-day decisions needed to be made by those closest to the point of action. In matters relating to curriculum, grading policies, and parental involvement, for example, those closest to the action have been given the authority to create cross-functional teams and develop recommendations for faculty review and action.

"I firmly believe we wouldn't be gathered together today to celebrate our achievements with our Governor and superintendent if we had not practiced what we preached and changed the way our school operated. Do you think we did the right thing?" the principal asked.

Applause erupted once again from the audience and as the principal left the podium and sat down, the audience continued to applaud. They spontaneously rose to their feet to show their appreciation of their beloved principal.

Mary, John, and Jerri sat transfixed as they watched the school assembly and could hear the roar of applause emanating from the crowd. As they watched the principal, each saw a tear streak down the side of the leader's face. The audience, too, saw the principal's reaction to their applause and clapped even louder. As they stood on their feet and cheered, even the Governor seemed overwhelmed by the respect these students and adults were showing for this person.

After the applause had continued for some time, another adult stood up and went to the podium. "As superintendent of our school system, I am so proud to be with you today and to share in your recognition and accomplishments. I could not be prouder of what has happened at this school, and I, too, want to say thanks to the administration, faculty, and student body for what you have taught me as superintendent and what we have learned as a school system from your actions.

"I remember well when your principal first came into the system," continued the superintendent. "There were other principals who did not take kindly to the new ideas being tried at Andrews, but over time, many of our principals began to learn from this school and changed the way they ran their schools accordingly. Let me give you one example.

"One of the ways teachers are more involved in this school's operations is through a program called peer coaching. Peer coaching involves teachers observing one another teaching and then discussing what went well and what could be improved. This strategy seemed like a radical idea to accomplish for your school and for our district goal of quality administrators and staff. However, over time, the results were successful and today all of the schools in our system but one have implemented this strategy. And it began right here at Andrews. Teachers here shared what they were doing with other teachers and then others expressed an interest to learn.

"So I congratulate you on your recognition of exemplary status, but I also thank you for helping all of us in this school system continuously improve our services to do the best job we can. You have led the way. Thanks!"

A thunderous applause broke out among the crowd, and a number of the adults sitting in the audience smiled with pride. These adults were the teachers who had implemented peer coaching and felt a great sense of pride that their efforts were helping others as well.

The next speaker began by saying; "As a member of the Andrews School Faculty, I too am very proud of what we have accomplished, and I want to share a few thoughts with you about how we have come so far over the past ten years.

"I was one of those faculty members that was around a long time ago when our principal first came, and believe me, I didn't like what was happening at first. But what really began to change my attitude was the accessibility of the administration. Through both philosophy and action, the administrators at Andrews have always been highly visible and actively involved in school and community issues. This administration has rarely asked us to do something they wouldn't do as well. And this has resulted in a spirit of teamwork and camaraderie that I never experienced before our principal came ten years ago.

"In all honesty, this idea of being accessible was a bit much at first. Our administration had us doing all kinds of things that were unheard of in previous years. Faculty, do you remember the first time we met with the staff of our neighboring feeder schools? Do you remember reviewing curriculum and discussing how we could correlate basic skills across grades and subject matter? Do you remember the dissension in our ranks when we began to do this?"

A low murmur spread throughout the gym.

"And do you remember when our entire faculty began visiting local employers regularly to learn firsthand the newest trends and skills needed in the future? I remember those first visits, and quite frankly I wasn't very happy about it. But today, all of us—teachers, cafeteria workers, guidance counselors, and custodians—meet with area employers all the time. I think this has been very important in the achievements of our school, and I hope our classes are more relevant and realistic to students than they used to be. Am I right?"

Applause rose again, this time from the students in the audience. It was evident to everyone in attendance, and those watching from above, that students really appreciated their faculty and the teaching-learning process in place at Andrews School.

"And finally, do you remember when the Andrews School Leadership Team, made up of faculty, students, and parents, was first put in place? Over the years we have looked at everything from student discipline to basic skills testing to the quality of the cafeteria food. I believe this Leadership Team has been instrumental in our success, because we really do own our school. And when you feel like something is a part of you, I believe you try even harder than ever before.

"I'm proud to represent the faculty today, but I'm even prouder that our hard work, dedication, and belief in ourselves have helped us become what we are today, a wonderful place to work and a wonderful place to learn. Thanks for all that you've done!

"At Andrews School we 'walk the talk,' and I've never been prouder to be an educator than I have during these last ten years."

Another thunderous round of applause erupted as the speaker left the podium.

As the applause began to die down, a young person wearing a "Spread the Word" T-shirt and blue jeans stepped up to the podium. This young person addressed the assembly by stating, "I really appreciate the chance to represent the student body at today's assembly. I am very proud of our school and want to begin by thanking the faculty and administration for giving us a voice.

"I know our school is not perfect, but I think the one thing we really have going for us is the respect we students have from our teachers and administrators. They will listen to us and give us a voice in what happens here. I especially like the chance we students have to share our thoughts and experiences with the community. Instead of the principal and teachers speaking to civic groups, we students get to speak in the community No one at this school is afraid of what we might say, because they know this school is ours and we are just as proud of it as they are.

"I also like the banner that is hung from the ceiling in the entrance to the school. The banner states, 'Doing your best isn't good enough if you don't know what you're doing.' I want to share my ideas about why I think this statement is so important.

"In many schools, decisions are made by the adults with little input from students. But in our school, we are driven to make decisions based on input and results. Our teachers don't do things just because they have always been done a certain way. They listen to us, we gather data, and changes are considered and made. Yes, we own this school just as much as anyone else, and I am proud that the voice of the student is important."

Another round of applause sounded as the student returned to his assigned seat, and the applause continued as a final speaker rose to address the audience.

"As president of the Parent-Teacher-Student Association, I couldn't be prouder of our school. I have had four children attend this school, and I have seen over the years a real change in how Andrews operates. Today's award is the culmination of those changes.

"The one thing I really appreciate is how important parents are to the welfare of our school. The idea that schools have customers, and that parents are important customers, is one of the greatest things that has happened at Andrews. Being viewed as an important part of the school, and being told that parents are important customers, is worth its weight in gold.

"I am not surprised by this award. I believe it begins with leadership. There is no substitute for leadership. And at Andrews, we have leaders everywhere—our administration, faculty, and students. With this kind of leadership in our school, higher performance is bound to occur. Leadership is the key to this award today.

"I also believe that the vision and mission of our school have helped guide us through the good times and difficult times. We know where we are going and have kept the faith

Riding the Wave

that our direction was the right course of action.

"I think that Andrews School has shown the world that with high expectations and a 'walk the talk' approach, anything is possible. I have felt for a long time that most parents, students, and educators have expected too little of our schools and the people who work in them. I am most proud that Andrews School expects so much of everyone, and all of us have delivered on those expectations. What a great place our school has become.

"Governor, I've never met parents that didn't care about their child and want the best for him or her. I've met a lot of parents who didn't know how to express or act upon their feelings, but that doesn't mean they didn't care just as much. I also believe that every community in this country wants their schools to be the best they can be, but often the community isn't invited to join the school team. If you really want to know why Andrews School is exemplary, you can throw those test scores out the window. Our school is great because we are united, we are customer driven, and all of us have the right and responsibility to join the vision of Andrews School as a member of the school team. That's why we are exemplary, and that's why we are here today. Thank you."

Once again applause broke out among the audience and as the assembly began to end, students and adults joined together in the middle of the assembly room where they talked, laughed, shook one another's hands, and engaged in animated, happy conversation.

John, Mary, and Jerri continued to watch the audience gathered in the middle of the floor. The three were overwhelmed by what they had just seen. As the screen began to fade, another scene formed before their eyes. A group of teachers were gathered in the teacher's lounge talking.

"There is another reason why we have been so successful," said one of the teachers. "When the principal began making all these changes ten years ago, there was an understanding that asking people to do things differently also required a great deal of professional development."

"Yes," stated another teacher. "All of us have been through one new program after another. And quite frankly, I thought at first the principal's approach was just another flavor of the month. I thought if we could just wait this out, it would go away."

"But we all knew this wasn't just another new program when the principal began to emphasize professional development to help us deal with the changes being proposed," added another teacher. "Do you remember all the grumbling among the faculty over all the staff development we had to go through?"

"My gosh," added still another teacher, "we were staff-developed to death. Just think of all that we went through. From training in teaching techniques to the deployment of high performance tools, we have been through more learning in the last few years than I ever went through even in college."

"It's one thing to have a mission and all that," added another, "but quite another to implement this vision through professional development. The principal is right. Having one without the other may contribute to short-term success, but probably leads to long-term failure. Our principal just wasn't going to lead this school into failure."

The scene then shifted to another location in the school.

In the basement, a man and a woman, both dressed as custodians, were sitting on a couple of chairs, surrounded by cleaning materials, mops, and boxes of paper.

"That was quite an event," said the man. "We really have a good school, don't we?"

"You bet we do, and I'm glad to be a part of this place," replied the lady. "We both know what it's like to work in a place where no one cared what you thought or did." She paused. "But it's not like that here. Why do you believe what we think is so important?"

"I can tell you one reason," replied the man. "Because, when they listen to us they save money. Do you remember the Christmas vacation four years ago when the boiler went out? All kinds of experts came here to tell us how much it was going to cost to replace the boiler. Finally, our principal turned to me and asked me what I thought.

"I figured the experts would have a heart attack when I told him that all we needed to do was take the old boiler out of that abandoned school across town and bring it over here and hook it up. Both of the boilers were of the same make and model, and there wasn't anything wrong with that other boiler."

"I remember that," replied the lady. "They did listen to you and switched them. The boiler from that abandoned school worked fine. I believe you saved the school system about $200,000. I guess now I see why they include us so much. They know we have something to say."

The scene changed again.

In a hallway, as students milled around in the background, a television camera was set up and a reporter was talking with the principal.

"What is the key message you would share with other schools and communities about your success?" the TV reporter asked.

"It's been said that just about every major problem facing public education in this country is being solved by some school somewhere 'out there'," the principal said, staring directly into the camera. "Success is not a secret. Instead, it takes a willingness to stick to an approach that combines leadership, knowledge, skills, and a long-term outlook that is unwavering. My message is simple: Andrews School is an example of how public education can and will work for the

Prologue

young people of our school. It's not magic. It's just practicing common sense."

⌢⌢⌢⌢⌢⌢

Mary, John, and Jerri sat in their respective locations trying to absorb all they had seen and heard. For each, the past few days became clear in both meaning and context. Questions about understanding the four bytes and eleven core values (discussed in *CommonSense.com*) were replaced with a deeper level of understanding about the concept of high performance. To discuss it theoretically was one thing, but to see it come alive in a real school was another factor altogether.

Mary, John, and Jerri, all educators in different locations across the country, contemplated their next steps. In a situation none of them totally understood, each had been given a unique opportunity to learn about education improvement from an unlikely source: the Internet.

During the past few weeks each had learned about ways to improve their education systems and had learned about the key values that help drive improvement. All maintained a level of frustration in their current jobs, but had learned that instead of placing blame on others, it was very important to fix the processes . . . to fix the system itself.

These words of wisdom had come through a chat room that mysteriously appeared on their computer screens, with the author someone (or something) called CommonSense.com. Andrews School was the culminating lesson learned . . . an application of all the principles and values discussed by John, Mary, and Jerri via CommonSense.com

As the three of them sat glued to their computer screens, a

message appeared from their unknown friend:

"I hope today's visit to Andrews School has helped you form a clear picture of high performance in education. Each of you has an important role to play, no matter what your position in your organization.

"I thank you sincerely for your willingness to learn new ideas, and I wish you the very best in your journey toward success and continuous improvement.

"It's not magic. It's just practicing common sense."

With that, their computer screens went blank.

ONE: A Challenge to Align
Aligned Management System

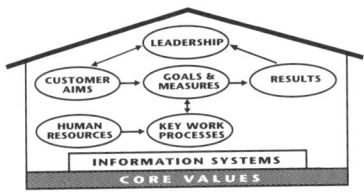

Mary, John, and Jerri considered what they had learned from CommonSense.com with a renewed sense of commitment and enthusiasm. Through the power of what seemed to them a magical technological resource—an omnipotent phantom chatroom contact—these three educators had been given the opportunity to renew themselves professionally and grow. This new learning perspective had helped them realize a deeper level of understanding about the concept of high performance. To discuss how to become a high performing organization had been one thing. To see its realization come alive in Andrews School was quite another. With the picture of the Andrews School assembly still vivid in their minds, each continued to study the core values learned from CommonSense.com.

During the coming weeks, they each went about improving their respective education systems. Mary, as a teacher, had begun to think about improving her classroom. John, as a principal, was busy generating ideas about improving his school. And Jerri, as a superintendent, was concentrating on improving her school district. The tension generated earlier by their job and career frustrations had lessened. Because of their contact with CommonSense.com, they now had a direction.

Riding the Wave

But each wanted more. The need to remain in contact was important. Video-cam and split-screen technology provided them an exciting avenue. Instead of losing interest, each felt a deep sense of inner conflict about wanting to know more. Each read a great deal of information about school improvement, yet it seemed as if what they read was more of the "same old stuff" that had been proposed for years but didn't seem to really make a difference. Each continued to read materials about quality, Baldrige, and other related topics. But each felt a sense of isolation without the direction provided previously by CommonSense.com. They missed the refreshing anticipation of CommonSense.com's presence. They missed the exhilaration of being challenged to think "outside the box," by their intriguing and wise chatroom companion. Like a pot sitting on a hot stove, each felt he or she might reach a boiling point out of frustration and what seemed like a thwarted desire to learn more. Unfortunately, it seemed their days of communicating about high performance with CommonSense.com were over.

During one especially bleak winter day, John, Mary, and Jerri met for their now regular weekly get-togethers. Even though they lived in different regions, each was feeling especially forlorn because of the gray skies and unusually cold temperatures across the country. Touching base felt like a good way to pass the time on a bleary day. All three were rather quiet and more contemplative than usual.

"Weather's terrible here," said Mary.

"Ditto, in my place," said John.

"Raining down here," said Jerri. "But not as cold as where you two are."

All three sat, just staring at their screens . . . staring at each other, embarrassed at their digression into mundane chitchat about the weather.

"Think we'll ever hear from CommonSense.com, again?"

Chapter One: A Challenge to Align

said John, suddenly broaching the subject all had been hesitant to bring up.

"I miss those sessions," said Jerri.

"I do, too," Mary said. "I think I'm really doing some good things in my classroom, right now, but . . ."

"But you've reached a point that you want more, haven't you?" said Jerri, interrupting Mary.

"You're right," said John. "I think that's what's been bothering me, too."

An uncomfortable silence fell over the three, once again. Each was waiting on the others for something—some thought, some idea, some direction—when suddenly a message began to emerge across each educator's screen.

"Do you see what I'm seeing?" said John.

"It's a message," said Mary, excitement in her voice.

"I see it, too," said Jerri, almost in a whisper.

The three educators waited breathlessly as the following message finally appeared in its entirety on their screens:

River of No Return

The Middle Fork of the Salmon River originates 20 miles north of Stanley, Idaho, and is formed by the merging of Bear Valley and Marsh Creeks. The 2.3 million-acre Frank Church River of No Return Wilderness, through which the river runs, includes parts of the Nezperce, Bitterroot, and Salmon National Forests. The River of No Return Wilderness has been set aside to preserve and perpetuate natural conditions. This wilderness is one of the most rugged, scenic, and isolated in the North American continent.

The message stayed just long enough to be read, then just as suddenly as it had appeared, it disappeared.

For a few brief moments, no one spoke.

"Think it was just some junk e-mail?" said Jerri, the first to break the silence.

"But would it have appeared on all our screens at the same time?" said John. "Just out of the blue? From Stanley, Idaho?"

"Don't you find it interesting that it appeared just after we had all shared some common frustrations?" said Mary.

"So," said John, "what do we do, now?"

"Wait," said Jerri.

"Wait," said Mary.

~~~~~~

So they waited. The next week's session couldn't come quickly enough. When the day arrived, all three gathered at the appointed time with great anticipation.

"Think we'll get a follow-up to the message?" asked John.

"I hope so," said Mary. "A message about a river in Idaho is a bit of a stretch."

"Was for me, too," said Jerri. "But if it truly was from CommonSense.com, a follow-up that helps to make a tie to a learning challenge will come."

And sure enough, John, Mary, and Jerri were not disappointed.

"Here it comes," said Mary.

The following message appeared across their screens:

Subject: The Sheepeaters

In the early 1800's, Shoshone Indians were found living in the Salmon River Mountains. This early discovery was confirmed later when bone chips, tools, and mussel shells were found in rock shelters along the rugged canyon walls. The Sheepeater Indians, a subgroup of the Northern Shoshone, depended on mountain sheep for food.

As settlers and cavalry infiltrated the territory of the Sheepeaters, a campaign to subdue these Shoshone Indians

Chapter One: A Challenge to Align

took place in 1879. Captain Bernard negotiated the surrender of the Sheepeaters—51 in all. The Indians had been worn out physically and psychologically by their pursuers.

"What an incredibly sad story," said Jerri.

"Worn out physically . . . and psychologically," said Mary. "Guess that's kind of like we're feeling, isn't it?"

"Yeah," said John, "pursued by mediocrity and 'business as usual.'"

"There must be a tie," said Jerri, "you know, to the river message."

"And maybe to . . ."

Just then, a second message interrupted Mary as it appeared across their screens.

Andrews School

"The pleasure of the place makes me think of John Stuart Mill, who was a philosopher specializing in happiness. He said, 'The main constituents of happiness appear to be two: Tranquility and excitement. With much tranquility they may find that they can be content with very little pleasure. With much excitement, they may reconcile themselves to a great deal of pain. If so, a good river must be essential happiness—happiness distilled and running between high banks, because on a river, tranquility and excitement alternate every half mile, every quiet pool.'

I think it is a pity that Mill, a 19th century philosopher, never found a way to run a desert river."

Kathleen Dean Moore

"Andrews School," said Mary, as if just continuing her earlier interrupted thought.

"Guess we're on our way to another learning adventure," said John. "But who is Kathleen Moore, and what does she

Riding the Wave

have to do with Andrews School?"

"I love this," said Mary. "The intrigue, the mystery, the challenge . . . These messages are somehow connected to our 'visit' to Andrews School. Don't know how or why, but there's some connection."

"Keeps my juices flowing," said John.

"Umm," said Jerri. "The challenge of new learning says something about learning for all of us, doesn't it? Adults and children."

"Yeah, a good river? Andrews School? Psychologically tired? The tranquility and excitement part fits." said Mary. "Wonder where this is going?"

"I've got a feeling we're going to find out," said John.

The following week, the three gathered in front of their computers.

"It's like a wonderful jigsaw puzzle, isn't it?" said John.

All three laughed. Suddenly, words appeared on their respective screens.

Aligned Management System

"Another piece," said Mary.

More words followed.

<u>Leadership</u>   <u>Aims</u>   <u>Goals and Measures</u>
<u>Information Systems</u>   <u>Key Work Processes</u>
<u>Human Resources</u>   <u>Results</u>

That was it—nothing but these words.

"Now we're getting somewhere," said Jerri. "Andrews School, Shoshone Indians and good rivers . . . and these terms. I know they are connected."

"Yes," said John, "familiar sounding terminology, isn't it?"

Chapter One: A Challenge to Align

"I think we're in for some new ways to look at them," said Mary.

"See you next week," said Jerri.

~~~~~~~~~

Next week couldn't come quickly enough for Jerri, John, and Mary. In fact, facing each other as they sat at their computers, they remained in silence. Too excited to talk with each other. The minutes that passed seemed like hours. And just when it seemed that this week would be absent a message, words suddenly appeared.

>Hello, John . . . Mary . . . Jerri

"I knew it," said Mary.

"Shhh," said Jerri.

"Finally," said John.

>Though we don't know each other personally, we have a mutual friend . . . CommonSense.com. I know you are in suspense, so I will get right to the point. This summer, you are invited, as special guests, to participate in a whitewater-rafting trip down the Middle Fork of the Salmon River. Think about it. All you have to do is arrange transportation to Stanley, Idaho, on the designated day; all other arrangements and expenses will be covered.
>
>Jim

The three friends sat in silence. None knew what to say. This invitation . . . from a stranger . . . out of the blue . . .

>I can tell from your lack of responses that you are having trouble with this invitation. Of course I understand. And besides, anything that seems to be free must have a catch. And there is one. You must be willing to learn. Other than that, there is no catch. You have been invited to participate

on this week-long rafting trip and your expenses have all been paid for up front. Now, what do you think?

"Who are you?" said Mary. It was John and Jerri's burning question, too.

Fair enough question. First, let me tell you that we four have a lot in common. I have a passion for education and young people. And I have spent many years in the frustrating world of trying to improve our schools. Today I continue to work in education during part of the year and do other things in the summer. In fact, I will be your guide on this trip . . . if you choose to go.

My life has been changed by the implementation of the seven categories of the Aligned Management System (AMS) listed for you in an earlier message. Because of my belief in continuous improvement, I have promised others and myself that I would share what I have learned. This is our connection to CommonSense.com . . . and you three are my "special projects" for this upcoming summer.

You have been offered this invitation for a reason. You have been taught the importance and power of reflection. The three messages—the river, the Shoshone Indians, Kathleen Dean Moore, along with Andrews School—give some fodder for reflection, wouldn't you say?

Now about the invitation. The real question is this: Are you willing to take a leap of faith and join me this summer? Think about it. I'll be back in touch in one week.

Jim

Just as suddenly as the message appeared, it ended.

"Either of you two ever been whitewater rafting?" asked Mary.

"I rowed a boat on a pond, once," said John.

"I rode on a ferryboat last year," said Jerri.

"So, any doubts about going on this trip?" asked John.

Chapter One: A Challenge to Align

"Plenty," said Mary.

"Let's give it a week's thought," said Jerri.

"I agree," John said.

Over the course of the week, John, Jerri, and Mary contemplated the invitation. The lure of the excitement of a rafting trip and the charismatic enigma of CommonSense.com, obviously working through this stranger, Jim, was strong. But each still struggled with that "leap of faith."

Mary had traveled rarely outside of her home state and had never flown in an airplane. To think of taking off by herself and flying to Idaho was frightening. *But I know I can do this,* thought Mary. *If I am ever going to continue to grow as an educator, I've got to learn more about school improvement than I presently know . . . and I'm sure not going to find it out just hanging around here.*

John had great difficulty taking a week off during the summer. As a principal, with student schedules to create and teaching assignments to be made, the summer was no less busy for him than other times of the year. He already was scheduled for a week's vacation with his family at the beach. How was he ever going to find time for another week away from home? And what would his family say about him disappearing by himself for a week? *Man, it's a risky venture, to put it mildly,* thought John. *But no pain . . . no gain. I just have to go on this trip to see if I can learn more.*

As a superintendent, being away from home was pretty common for Jerri, and she had promised her husband and kids that this summer would be different—that her schedule would be reduced, and she would have more time at home. To take off for Idaho would violate this promise. But she discussed the dilemma with her husband.

"Jerri," he said, "you have been looking for answers to improve your profession ever since I've known you. Now you have a chance to perhaps learn a great deal that would help you achieve this goal. You can't say no to this trip."

Should I go for it? thought Jerri.

Waiting for the week to end seemed like forever for John, Mary, and Jerri. But as soon as they logged onto their computers, a message was waiting.

Greetings. What is your decision?

"I'm in," typed John.

"Me, too," typed Jerri.

"Ditto," typed Mary.

Wonderful, wonderful. I am excited that all of you have agreed to go. You are in for a breathtaking adventure. Along the way, you will learn about the seven categories of the Aligned Management System (AMS). And you will learn something about yourselves—as individuals ... as educators. Remember the time you spent learning about the core values? The power of your commitment to understanding the core values, in conjunction with new learnings about the Aligned Management System, will be nothing short of transformational. I guarantee! Now, you are thinking ... details, right?

These will arrive in good time for you to make arrangements.

Take care,

Jim

Abruptly, their screens went blank.

"Whew, I'm kind of breathless," said Jerri.

"You're telling me," said John. "Rafting on a river—obviously a metaphor for the learning journey we will be taking this summer."

"Look," said Mary, interrupting. "There's something more on our screens."

Sure enough, each of the three screens began to fill once

again. This time . . . the words that began to scroll across the screen were accompanied by music.

"The River," all three said, in unison.

"By Garth Brooks," said John.

"I love that song," said Mary.

"I think I'm going to write down the words," said Jerri.

The three friends listened as the words about dreams and daring . . . destination and trying flowed melodically through their computer speakers.

"I've got a feeling that listening to and studying the lyrics of this song is our 'homework' between now and our departure," said John, as the song ended. "You know . . . how it relates to us as leaders in education . . . and as a person."

"Good ol' CommonSense.com," said Jerri. "Just like our friend to challenge us with something thought-provoking."

"Think CommonSense.com is really Jim?" said Mary.

"Could be," said John.

"Could be," said Jerri.

TWO: A Dream Is Like a River
Aligned Management System

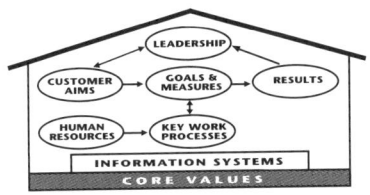

Details. Prior to the beginning of summer, the three educators received airline information, a clothing and supply list, a book on whitewater rafting explaining the various levels (classes) of rapids, and a map with a detailed explanation of the Salmon River. The Whitewater Rafting Company was to be their "outfitter," a term used for the company serving as guide, cook, and all-around organizer for a rafting trip. They also found out that Stanley, Idaho, was a quaint town with a few shops, restaurants, and motels.

Midsummer couldn't arrive quickly enough for the three educators. But arrive it did. A July 4th week on a river in Idaho. A chance to see each other in person. And the opportunity to continue to grow and learn how to do their jobs better. The anticipation made school closing for summer both exhilarating and never-ending for John, Jerri, and Mary.

The airport, late afternoon, at Boise, Idaho. Hugs, high fives, and comparing newly purchased gear were the order of the day. Seeing each other, in person, was so much better than the image of each other in the video-cam. After the initial

Riding the Wave

greetings were over, John, Mary, and Jerri gathered at a sign that said:

> **The River of No Return Group**
>
> **Whitewater Rafting Company**

"Looks like us," said Jerri.

The three were directed to a specific location along the walkway of the ground transportation area at the airport. A representative from the Whitewater Rafting Company was waiting. So, with gear and luggage tossed in the bed of a muddied, extended-cab truck, Jerri, Mary, and John made the hour drive up the mountain to a tiny lodge in Stanley, Idaho.

Upon arrival, the three tired travelers went immediately to their respective rooms. According to the itinerary information, they were to report at 8:00 a.m. the next morning for a meeting in the motel lobby. But a restful sleep escaped all three. The day's travel had wearied them, but the questions, issues, and excitement about the morning made sleep almost impossible. They knew the upcoming river trip would be an adventure, yet each still harbored worries about what the adventure would bring.

The next morning at eight, the three educators joined twelve other "adventurers." All were loaded on an old school bus for a three-hour twisting and turning bus trip up to Boundary Creek Camp and the Launch Area. Whitewater Rafting Company's assistant guide, Meg, pointed out especially wonderful views and majestic landmarks. A mountain range, still snow-capped even in July. Powder puff clouds drifting silently in a brilliant blue sky. Rich green meadows, forests, and foliage—evidence of abundant rain during the past few months.

Chapter Two: A Dream Is Like a River

"Check out the wildflowers," said Meg. "And the rock formations. And don't forget to take a look at the lakes and rivers that we pass."

"This place is gorgeous," said Jerri. But as she stared through the dusty bus window, Jerri began to hear music. Music from a now very familiar song.

"Garth," said John.

Mary had brought a small battery-operated CD player. Turning up the volume, Mary, along with John, Jerri, and the other passengers, listened to the haunting lyrics of the song.

Jerri began to think of her role as a leader and the challenge to take risks. To find a better way, no matter how rough things might be. *This trip is about this song,* she thought. *Being involved . . . and daring to reach for new levels of personal and professional improvement and satisfaction. That's what I have to do.*

Mary's thoughts drifted in a different direction. Always one who appreciated nature, Mary was struck by the majesty of the scenery, the soaring mountain peaks and quiet beauty of a place where the only sounds were birds and animals communicating to one another in their natural habitat. *If only my students could see this,* she thought. *The sky out here must go on forever. Oh, what they could learn.* Then she smiled to herself. *Oh, what I could learn.*

John thought about Jim. He liked Jim, even though he had never seen him. But there was something about him. He just knew that Jim was a very special person who was going to help them in much the same way as CommonSense.com had done previously. He **must** be *CommonSense.com,* thought John. He remembered Jim's words, too. *And you will learn something about yourselves . . . as individuals . . . as educators.*

After a lengthy drive along this paved road, the bus pulled off the main highway onto a dirt road.

"We have left the low country and civilization behind," said Meg. "When we turned off the main highway onto this

Riding the Wave

dirt road, we left the world as you know it. Now, we are in the Challis National Forest and will arrive at our launch site in a little while."

This final dirt road leg of the journey through the Challis National Forest, with its switchbacks, potholes, and fallen rocks and limbs, left them all breathless. Finally, the bus driver parked and set the emergency brake at the launch site sign:

**Boundary Creek Camp and Launch Area
(US Forest Service-Idaho)**

But as soon as they disembarked, the riders were met by a second sign:

**You have reached the launch site
for a wild and scenic river—the
Middle Fork of the Salmon River.
Do not attempt to travel on the river
without qualified guides and
appropriate equipment.**

DANGER

**Anyone who does not follow all rules
and regulations regarding whitewater rafting
may suffer serious injury or death.**

**BE SAFE
AND HAVE FUN!**

As John, Mary, and Jerri exited the bus, they glanced nervously at one another.

"Umm," said Jerri, "Be safe and have fun. Do both of those things go together?

Chapter Two: A Dream Is Like a River

"Sounds like what I tell my students on opening day," Mary said. Jerri and John laughed and agreed it sounded like a familiar opening day speech for them, as well.

"Being constantly safe is certainly an aim of mine," said John.

"Might make the fun part happen a little better, too," said Jerri.

Meg overheard the conversation and saw the nervous looks.

"Don't let the danger sign frighten you," she said. "But you should remember to respect the river at all times. You will be safe if you listen, learn the skills we will teach you, always think ahead, and trust one another. Hang in there. Once we get on the water, your fears will disappear."

"Welcome to the Whitewater Rafting Company," said a voice. The three educators and their twelve companions turned at the sound. A tall, tanned, middle-aged man, wearing a cowboy hat, t-shirt, and shorts approached the group.

"Folks," said Meg, "this is Jim. He's our lead guide for the upcoming trip."

"Thanks, Meg," said Jim. "Along with Meg and our other guide here, Tuck, I want to officially welcome you to Idaho and to the Middle Fork of the Salmon River. As I know you've already discovered, you all have varied backgrounds as well as a range of experiences with whitewater rafting. For some of you, this will be a new experience. I know some of you already consider yourselves experts. But no matter what your background or experience, we will consider ourselves a team. Everyone will have an important role . . . working together to have a safe, fun, one hundred mile, seven-day adventure on the river." He looked around the circle of faces before him. "Now, let me ask each of you—name one thing you would like to experience on this journey down the river."

"Make it back safe and sound," said Mary.

"See some beautiful sights," added Jerri.

Riding the Wave

"Be successful at doing something I've never done, before," said John. Others in the group named such things as "Do some fishing. Go hiking. Relax and reflect. Be challenged. Make some new friends" . . . and even, "Go one-on-one with the river, in a kayak."

Jim listened closely to all the responses, briefly conferred with Meg and Tuck, and then turned back to the group.

"That's a great list," he said. "Now let me respond. Many of your personal goals we have anticipated because of our past experience with groups, and we have customized for these things. You'd be surprised at the similarities there are among all the groups we get to work with. Some activities will be optional, and some we will do—depending upon time, weather, and absence of delays. Others will depend on your successes and your experiences—how quickly you learn and adapt—and on unexpected opportunities along the way. Periodically, we will assess how we are doing—ask your opinions . . . check on making sure we are meeting your needs." He removed his hat and ran his fingers through his hair. "One thing to remember: Everything we do is driven by the safety factor. In other words, 'Safety first—above all.'"

"Don't forget the fun part," said John.

Everyone in the group chuckled.

"You got it," said Jim.

And so, for the remainder of the morning and into the early afternoon, the "River Rats," the name coined by the group, immersed themselves into learning basic safety, boating, and paddling rules associated specifically with whitewater rafting. Life vests and helmets were non-negotiable regulation gear and "knowing" the river prior to rafting it was crucial. Jim asked them to pull out the European Rapid Rating System sheet they had all received prior to coming on the trip. He, along with Meg and Tuck, spent a great deal of time reviewing and explaining the levels.

Chapter Two: A Dream Is Like a River

"**Class I, Very Easy**," said Jim. "These have small regular waves and riffles, with very few obstacles."

"**Class II, Easy**," said Meg. "These rapids are made up of small waves with some eddies, low ledges, and slow rock gardens."

"**Class III, Medium**," said Tuck. "Numerous waves make up these rapids. They are high and irregular, with strong eddies. The passages are clear but narrow and they require expertise in maneuvering; even some scouting from shore is necessary."

"**Class IV, Difficult**," said Jim. "These are long rapids with powerful, irregular waves. There will be some dangerous rocks and boiling eddies. Precise maneuvering and scouting from the shore is imperative. All safety precautions are a must."

"**Class V, Very Difficult**," said Meg. "These are long rapids, too. But with wild turbulence and extremely congested routes that require complex maneuvering. These are definitely a danger to your life and boat. In fact, they are very close to the extreme limits of navigation."

"Finally," Tuck said, "There are the **Class VI, The Limits of Navigation** rapids. These are rarely run—and a definite hazard to your life."

"All right," said Jim, "now that we've put a bit of the fear of God into you, how about taking a look at this Panel Location Map that Meg and Tuck are handing out?"

The map depicted the entire seven-day trip. In addition, each member of the group received a map specifically describing the various rapids to be encountered, various points of interest for viewing along the way, and available campsites for anticipated rest and relief. Names of rapids like Sulphur Slide Rapid (**Class III**), the Chutes (**Class III+**) and Powerhouse Rapids (**Class IV**) did little to allay the fears of those with little experience. Yet for John, Mary, and Jerri, their fears were juxtaposed with the excitement of the challenge to succeed and accomplish . . . the challenge to work, think, and learn together to solve an "opportunity."

And before long, the initial training came to an end.

"We've given you the basics," Jim told them. "We've laid out the planned goals and activities and the optional ones. Each of you has had a chance to talk with us about your fears, your previous experiences or lack of them, any specific individual goals you would like to accomplish, and you've had a chance to meet and get to know one another. From here on out you will learn from experience and through applying what you've been taught to new situations—and by listening to each other."

The River Rats were ready to begin the first day's adventure, thirteen miles from the origin of the Middle Fork to their campsite, Scout Camp.

While all the rafters were making final preparations for boarding the three rafts, Jim suddenly approached John, Mary, and Jerri. He pulled them aside.

"So," he said, quietly to them. "Are you ready to live the song? Will you paddle your rafts until there is no longer any water in the river?" And then he winked.

"We wondered when . . ." said Mary.

"When I was going to 'get more to the point' about this trip?" Jim said, interrupting Mary.

"You're really . . . him . . . aren't you?" John asked.

"CommonSense.com?" said Jim, interrupting.

"It's you," said Mary.

"Sorry to disappoint you," said Jim, laughing, "but I'm just Jim, lead guide at Boundary Creek Camp."

"Oh, you're more than that," Jerri said with assurance.

"Remember when I told you I was in education?" Jim asked. "And that I truly believed in continuous improvement? Well, I know that you're three educators who want to learn more, aren't you?"

Chapter Two: A Dream Is Like a River

"Why, yes," said Mary, "but . . . "

"And you needed something—a challenge—something that would test you, keep you learning about yourselves and help you understand how to make a difference."

"You're right," said Jerri, "but . . ."

"And you've already learned a great deal about what it takes to create a high performing system."

"Yes, we have," said John, "but . . ."

"But you're not quite sure how it all goes together and the importance of the interrelationship and alignment of all the pieces."

"Yes, all of that is correct," said Mary.

"But it doesn't explain how you know so much about us," said Jerri.

"Unless *you* are CommonSense.com," added John.

"CommonSense.com isn't a '*you*'" Jim said, "but an '*is*.' And all I can tell you is that I am here to help you learn to 'ride the waves' of this whitewater river system." He grinned at them. "And hey, I'm still learning, too. The day I think I know everything there is to know about the river and rafting, that's the day I hope somebody tells me to hang it up, because that's the day the river will show me no mercy."

John, Jerri, and Mary turned to look at each other. As they did, they smiled.

"We're ready," they said, in unison.

"Good," said Jim, "let's get launched."

THREE: Leadership
Aligned Management System

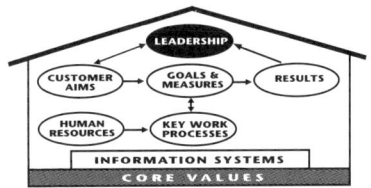

The fifteen River Rats, three guides, and three rafts launched from the dock at Boundary Creek, and moved into the river which was fairly narrow and shallow at this point. John and Mary were initially assigned to one of the paddle rafts, each of which was led by a guide, while Jerri took a turn, along with two other members of the group, riding in the oar raft—the one holding most of the group's provisions. One of the guides controlled this raft with a long, sweeping oar positioned at the stern. All rafters would eventually take turns riding in this one for brief rests from the arduous paddling in the other two rafts.

Getting to know the equipment and practicing for upcoming rapids was important for the first few miles. All rafters in the paddle rafts needed to become efficient at oar use. Learning was not difficult, especially if all on board followed the guide's directions at all times. "Left, right, stop, and move" became familiar words.

During their meandering down the seemingly quiet river toward the unrevealed ferocity of the upcoming rapids, John, Mary, and Jerri had the opportunity for brief discussions.

"This is going to be a great trip," said Mary, turning

toward John, who was sitting across from her.

"I'm really looking forward to the challenge of the rapids," John remarked as he deftly broke the rippling surface of the water with his paddle.

"Journey," said a voice from one of the other rafts.

"Huh?" said John, turning to see Jim's oar raft come alongside.

"Mary said 'trip'," said Jim. "To me it's more than that."

"It's a journey, isn't it?" said Jerri, sitting across from Jim.

"What's the difference?" asked Mary, as she boated her paddle.

"In short, a trip is a one-time experience," said Jim. "But a real journey is continuous and ever-changing."

"A journey is like a river," John said. "It's always flowing here and there . . . turning bends in forking. . . traveling along changing shorelines."

"And learning," added Jerri, "is what we do along the way . . . sort of the raft we travel in . . . you know?"

"That's a bit of a paraphrase, isn't it?" said Mary.

"Yeah," said John, smiling, "I guess it is."

"But an appropriate one," Jim said. "Sounds like you guys have been thinking about the song."

The three friends looked at each other and smiled.

Jim smiled too, and then got everyone's attention. "All right, listen up, all you River Rats," he said, as the rafts dipped and the water slapped the heavy gauge rubber, "Our first rapids will be on us pretty quickly."

"That's Velvet Falls, right?" asked Jerri, studying her maps. "And I believe they are a Class IV rapid."

"Well done, Jerri," Jim said, smiling approval at Jerri's obvious commitment to learn and to use the information they had been provided. "Using what we know about the rapids will help us to do what better?"

"Be safe!" shouted John.

Chapter Three: Leadership

"Have fun!" added Mary.

"Absolutely," said Jim. "As Jerri said, we're getting ready to hit Velvet Falls, one of the trickiest rapids on the river. You won't be able to hear Velvet Falls because of the Class II rapid at the beginning of this section of the river."

"And that's why it's called Velvet Falls," added Meg.

"Look for a very large boulder about ten feet high and twenty feet long," continued Jim. "The falls are about twenty feet below this boulder, so use it as a point of origin when you begin."

"When Jim uses the word 'falls'," Tuck said, "this is where the Class IV rapid comes into play. "It's really a giant drop into a very narrow channel. We'll need to stay to the left, right next to the boulder."

"I still find it hard to believe that one paddle can make a difference in such rough water," said Mary.

"By itself it's just flapping in the water," said Jim. "But each one of you is assigned a spot . . . a position. Look, just think of yourselves and your raft teammates as a part of a rafting system. You are a component in that system. And you are the leader in the position you hold. Your guide may be the leader of the boat. But he—pardon me, Meg—or she can't do all the paddling while everyone else goes along for the ride. The raft cannot be safely controlled and reach its destination without each of you playing a key role."

"That's right," added Meg. "You all know where we're going, right? Tuck, Jim and I—and now you—know something about Velvet Falls. Didn't we set and communicate directions for you?" Meg paused. "Now, one more time, everyone here knows that the group's goals are . . . what?"

"To make it through the rapids safely," said John.

"And to have fun doing it," said Mary.

"You guys are great," said Meg. "And our task is to keep you focused on those goals . . . give you directions based on

Riding the Wave

our knowledge and experience. We've taught you how to paddle, taught you about currents and turbulence, and all about rock ledges and boiling eddies."

"Meg's right," said Jim. "It's time to put that training to the test. You all did very well in the practice and learning earlier today. I have faith in you. Just remember—and I can't stress this enough—listen to each other, concentrate on your job, and translate what you have learned into positive decisions."

"Well, I'm ready to hit it," Tuck said. "And I think my group is chomping at the bit, right team?"

"Go, go, go!" shouted the River Rats assigned to Tuck's raft.

"Let's do it, then," said Jim, pushing off from the other two rafts. "And after we shoot the rapid, we'll gather together to talk about it."

Within a few minutes, the first of the three rafts had entered and successfully navigated the Class II rapid and moved past the large boulder. And soon, as directed by the guides, each raft worked its way successfully down the left side, steering clear of the shallow areas which were hiding numerous rocks. Deft paddle thrusts cut through chopping white foam. Showers of white water spray doused the focused and intense rafters. And then, after what seemed like an eternity, it was suddenly over—in thirty seconds.

A rousing cheer of relief rose from the River Rats on all three rafts, as they floated easily in the quiet eddy below and just beyond the rapid.

"We made it!" shouted John.

"Well done," Jim told them, directing his raft alongside Tuck's.

"Whew!" said Mary, "I can't believe it. I'm actually sitting in a raft, soaking wet I might add, that made it through . . . through that." She pointed back toward the rushing waters

Chapter Three: Leadership

behind them.

"Let's analyze that just a bit, Mary, now that we've finally shot a rapid, together," said Jim, looking at the exhausted yet exhilarated River Rats. "Do you know why you made it?" he asked.

"We worked as a team," offered John. "Everyone paddled in the same direction."

"We remembered—and used—what you taught us," said Jerri. "And when Meg shouted 'Stay left!' we did."

"We're the best!" announced Mary, suddenly, her face beaming.

Jim, Meg, and Tuck laughed.

"You're the best paddler sitting in your seat that you know, aren't you, Mary?" said Jim, still smiling. He looked around at each of them. "Each raft crew knew where we were going, your guide kept you focused on the task at hand, and you found out every paddler was necessary . . . thus you experienced success. Now, can you take what you learned from what you just did and do it again?"

"Bring on those rapids," said John, lifting his paddle into the air.

"That's the spirit," said Jim.

And for the remainder of the first day's journey, the River Rats alternately shot Class II and III rapids and then meandered along stretches of lazy, deeper river. They marveled at seemingly topless soaring ponderosa pines, dizzying rocky cliff ledges reachable only by eagles, and the sheer magnitude of their own personal and group successes . . . and near misses.

Just as the River Rats observed the sun start to creep below the horizon, they eased their rafts to the shores of Scout Camp, in a timbered section of a jutting bar.

"Oh, my aching back," said John, as he scrambled over the raft's gunwale and into the shallow water at the river's edge.

"Me, too," Jerri said, sloshing through the ankle-deep

Riding the Wave

water and up onto the sandy beach, "but it's a good ache, because we worked hard and were successful."

"Hey . . . we even got better as we went along," said Mary, removing her life jacket and spreading it out to dry.

"Yeah," said John, "meeting after each rapid to discuss how we did really helped."

"C'mon," said Mary, "let's go see what we can do to help set up camp."

"I've got a feeling that the eating and sleeping will be a lot better if we do," added John.

They spent the remainder of the afternoon, under the direction of Jim, Meg, and Tuck, helping to organize the camp for maximum comfort and efficiency. Every River Rat had a stake in effectively setting up the camp and participating in meal preparation and clean up.

After dinner, John, Mary, and Jerri took a stroll to the end of the bar. John reached into his pocket and pulled out a piece of paper.

"What's that?" asked Jerri.

"Remember when 'Aligned Management System' appeared on our screens," he said.

"Sure," said Mary. "There was a list of seven terms associated with it."

"Well, I wrote them down," said John.

Mary leaned over John's shoulder and began reading out loud, "Leadership, Aims, Goals and Measures, Results, Key Work Processes, Human Resources, Information Systems."

Jim, who had been eavesdropping on their conversation, smiled.

"Umm, that list looks familiar."

"Oh, hi, Jim," said John. "Didn't see you standing there."

"First word on that list is Leadership," said Jim.

"Yeah," said Jerri, "and I think we saw some interesting examples of that today."

Chapter Three: Leadership

"Share with me," Jim suggested.

"I was particularly impressed with the respect we received," said Jerri, "from all three of you."

"The evidence of teamwork was especially impressive," Mary said. "Made for great efficiency. And I felt like I was part of the team, too."

"I noticed something of particular interest," said John. "You guys acted more like coaches—like facilitators, you know? Even though I knew you were 'in charge,' I really didn't feel like you were these unforgiving dictators."

"We weren't the only leaders, though, were we?" Jim asked them.

"You're right," said Jerri. "I felt like a leader, too. In fact, you made me feel like a leader . . . you know . . . when we helped set up camp. When you asked me to be responsible for organizing the clearing of areas for sleeping, I felt . . . in charge of that. And I hadn't thought of it until just now."

"You did that for each one of us, didn't you?" said Mary.

"Leadership in any organization is found at all levels of the organization," said Jim. "A successful rafting 'journey' won't happen if just the guides play all the leadership roles. Mary, remember when I said you were the best paddler in your seat?"

"Yes," said Mary.

"You were the leader in that seat," said Jim. "And if you had not done all you could to be the best paddle leader in your seat, our ride down that rapid would not have been as successful. In fact, it could have been disastrous."

"Not something we always recognize in education," John told them.

"Well," said Jim. "In education, leadership is not just principals and superintendents and directors and such."

"Let me get this right," said Mary. "You're saying that, in order to be truly successful, I have to look at myself as a leader, too, not just as one of the 'worker bee' teachers."

Riding the Wave

"You are the leader of your classroom system," said Jim. "Don't ever forget that."

"Then each of us, as leaders," said Jerri, "must be responsible for setting and communicating direction. Right?"

"Dead right," said Jim. "Future improvement counts on it—depends on it."

"But that means that students have some responsibility, too," John said. "Aren't they the leaders of their own learning systems? I mean, we are sort of like the 'students' here, but we've played a major leadership role in our own learning. You guys communicated clear directions . . . and then we acted upon them."

"Now you're really seeing the crucial role leadership plays," said Jim, "and the incredible importance of recognizing that leadership must be acknowledged as existing at all levels of the organization."

"Hey," said Mary, "I don't know about you guys, but I think it's time to act as leader of my 'sleep system.' If I'm going to risk the rapids and tiptoe with the tide tomorrow, then I'm going to hit the sack."

Jim, John, and Jerri laughed. The day had been a full one.

Chapter Three: Leadership

To Think About – Leadership

The first category of the Aligned Management System is LEADERSHIP. Without question, leadership must set the direction of the organization and monitor/communicate that direction. This involves goals, measures, and results, and is considered part of the strategic operation of the system. Leadership is found at all levels of the education system, and, therefore, each component of the system . . . learner, classroom, school, school district, and state . . . must apply this concept for long-term improvement to occur.

❏ Have you involved people who work in the system and those who receive the services of the system in setting and communicating direction?

❏ Do you work continually to improve leadership?

❏ Do you, as the leader, set and communicate direction regularly?

CommonSense.com

FOUR: Customer Aims
Aligned Management System

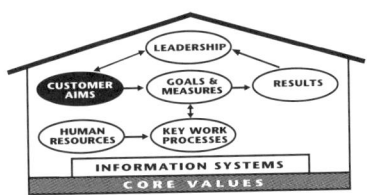

"Wake up, you lazy River Rats!"

"Huh," John grumbled, his sleepy face thrusting through the flaps of his one-man tent. "Didn't we go to sleep just a few minutes ago?"

"Up and at 'em," Jim called, wandering among the tents, as sleepy and sore adventurers emerged like moths from their cocoons.

"I think every bone in my body hurts," said Mary, barely peeking her head out. "Can't we sleep a bit longer?"

"Yeah," echoed Jerri, laughing. "We're the customers here, aren't we? You know, always right?"

"Right," said John, chiming in. "And as your customers, we've decided that we don't need to get up just yet."

"Oh," Jim said with a laugh, "and I suppose you'd tell your dentist that pain inside your back molar is nothing." Jim paused. "We believe our customers are always first . . . not necessarily always right. There's a difference."

"He's got us there," said Mary.

"The quicker you get those muscles moving, the quicker they'll warm up and the quicker the soreness will go away," Meg told them as she helped Jim roust out the rafters.

"Umm," said Jerri, turning toward the campfire where Tuck was leaning over a large skillet. "What's that wonderful smell?"

"Part of the fun," said Tuck, flipping the sizzling bacon that sputtered and crackled in the large cast-iron skillet hovering over the flames.

"Can we help?" asked Mary, who, along with the other campers, forgot her sore back and focused on the irresistible aroma mingling fresh pine and frying bacon.

"Sure," Tuck answered. "Pancake batter needs mixing and eggs need cracking in that big bowl there."

Soon, all the River Rats were busy helping Tuck with breakfast, and it wasn't long before he announced, "Come 'n' get it!" They all ate their fill of thick, crisp bacon, cheesy scrambled eggs, plump pancakes covered in butter and real maple syrup, and hot, dark coffee, brewed from cold, spring water.

"Wonder what's on CNN this morning?" John remarked after downing the last swallow of coffee in his cup and wiping his mouth on his sleeve.

"Whatever it is, it can't match what we're seeing up here," said Jerri. Her eyes surveyed the mountains in the distance, whose white snowcaps sparkled in the brilliant light of the early morning sun. Her gaze shifted to the nearby straight, brown trunks and brilliant green needles of the junipers surrounding the campsite by the river.

Meg, who was drying a cooking pot, eased beside Jerri. "Being able to look at all this is one of the reasons why I stay up here and work for Jim," she said.

"Does it ever get old?" asked Jerri.

"When I signed on with Jim, I told him that being close to nature was important to me. That if I took this job, I didn't want it to be 'just a job.' I'm good at what I do but . . ."

"But you wanted what you do to be good for you, too."

Chapter Four: Customer Aims

Both Meg and Jerri turned to see Jim approaching.

"You still remember that I said that, don't you?" said Meg, laughing.

"I'll never forget it," Jim said. "I think you interviewed me as much as I interviewed you that day. 'If I'm going to work for you,' you said, 'there are some things I need and expect.'"

"And you listened to me," said Meg. "You knew I had some specific aims, and . . . you listened."

"Yeah," chimed in Tuck with a smile. "Jim's funny like that. He doesn't want just you River Rats to have fun. He actually wants the experience to be fun for us, as well."

"Tuck's right," said Meg. "Sometimes he even lets us be right about something, doesn't he, Tuck?"

"Yep," agreed Tuck. "A good example is this place. Remember, Jim? Last year, Meg was the one that suggested this site would be better for our first overnight stop on the river. You wanted to go on down another couple of miles to camp at that . . . uh, well, how do I say it? Less desirable spot?"

"Well, I have to admit," said Jim, "Meg scouted out both sites, and her . . . uh . . ."

"Data was irrefutable. Is that what you mean, Jim?" said Tuck, interrupting Jim and laughing.

"Let's just say sleeping beneath a hornet's nest wasn't quite what I think you River Rats had in mind," said Jim.

"Sounds like Jim listens to you two quite a bit," said Mary.

"Jim's our leader," Meg told them, "but he wants us to work as a team. He talks with us, and he listens to us. It's how we decide what to do."

"Keep talking like that and I'll have to up my hat size," said Jim, taking off his cowboy hat and taking playful swipes at both Meg and Tuck. "Now, everyone, Meg and Tuck will demonstrate proper procedures on how to break camp, then I want us all to gather around in a circle on the beach for a briefing session."

"Jerri," whispered Meg, pulling the superintendent aside. "You asked me if this place ever gets old?"

"I think I already know the answer," said Jerri. Meg just smiled, and then moved to get with Tuck to coordinate the breaking of camp.

John, Mary, and Jerri finished packing up their tents and policing the area, then headed for the beach debrief area.

"Sounds like Meg and Tuck feel they have a real voice in how decisions are made, doesn't it?" said Mary, noticing the other members of the group gradually making their way into the debriefing circle. Soon, the entire group sat together on logs at the edge of the river. Jim, Meg, and Tuck were the last to join them.

"All right," Jim said. "Before we tackle the river today, I want us to look back at yesterday a bit. Talk about what went well, what can be improved. And I also want to revisit your list of needs and goals. Anybody remember what drives everything we do?"

"Safety first," offered Mary.

"Right," said Jim. "And John, what's another?"

"Fun," John answered.

"Anyone else?" asked Jim.

"Teamwork," one of the group said.

"Quality stuff to do," said another.

"You guys are quick," said Jim. "Remember when you talked about wanting to fish, see beautiful sights, do something you've never done and be successful, relax, be challenged, make new friends, go kayaking by yourself . . . remember?"

"Yeah," said Jerri, "you asked us for . . . uh . . . well, for lack of a better term . . . for our own aims for the trip."

"Well, the reason I went into this summer business was to make sure those kinds of things happen for folks like you," said Jim. "Meg and Tuck can speak for themselves, but I

Chapter Four: Customer Aims

happen to know that's also the key reason why they are here, as well."

"I'm here because you're such a great boss," said Tuck, smiling slyly and placing his hand over his heart. "I swear."

"You guys see what I have to put up with, don't you?" said Jim, frowning, but with a sparkle in his eyes.

"Now, it's important for you to know two filters that Meg, Tuck, and I must always keep in mind when we plan these trips for our customers. You know, filters that help us determine what we do while we're out here." Jim paused. "I just alluded to one. Care to guess what it is?"

"I'd say it has to do with why you're in the business," said Jerri. "You know, what you hope to see accomplished."

"Can you guess what the other one is?"

"Got to be your experience and expertise," said John.

"Exactly," said Jim. "When you tell me your goals, I have to decide, along with Meg and Tuck's input, which are appropriate and which are not."

"You know, your 'come back' when I joked about customers always being right this morning was interesting," said Jerri. "Sets up a bit of a different slant on things for me, and actually helps to validate some feelings I've always had when working with school boards and parents and such. Sometimes they ask for things that are just not the right thing to do."

"I think I know what you mean," said John. "Sometimes parents ask for things I know aren't good for their kids." John hesitated. "And I don't mean any disrespect, Mary, but teachers . . ."

"I know, I know," said Mary. "Sometimes we do the same thing. Not seeing the big picture can create problems, but those individual needs are still real—at least in the eyes of my fellow teachers." She paused. "And in my eyes, too."

"How do you know when those things they ask for are not the right thing?" asked Jim.

"It's the filters you mentioned that you use, isn't it?" said Jerri. "What you want to accomplish. That's one."

"And your experience and expertise," added Mary. "That's the other one."

"Right," said Jim, "if those of us in leadership positions followed the 'customer is always right' rule, everybody would get the idea that they could do everything they wanted at anytime, regardless of any consideration of the consequences. Now let me give you a great, personal example."

"Uh oh," whispered Meg, loud enough for the whole group to hear, "here comes *the* story."

Jim grinned, but ignored Meg's jibe.

"Before I took over here, another very competent guide was in charge. But the reason he's no longer here is the result of a poor decision he made *not* to apply our two filters. He chose to make his decision based on the old 'bottom line'."

"Money?" said John.

"Money," said Jim. "Higher profits . . . at any cost."

"What happened?" asked Jerri.

"A member of one of the rafting groups had a personal goal of going one-on-one with the river, and not just any rapid but a difficult one."

"And he let him?" asked a rafter.

"Sure did," said Jim. "The guy, who, by the way, was not an experienced kayaker, said he'd drop out of the group if he wasn't allowed. So, instead of staying true to the real purpose of this rafting business—providing folks a fun and safe adventure—he let this guy run a very dangerous rapid alone." Jim turned to Meg and said, "Tell 'em about Pistol Creek Rapid, Meg."

"Pistol Creek Rapid is a Class III to IV rapid," began Meg. "As you enter the rapid there is an immediate S turn that is extremely difficult. It's crucial that rafters approach Pistol Creek from the correct direction, which is from the left."

Chapter Four: Customer Aims

"The hole," said Tuck. "Don't forget the hole."

"Tuck's right," said Meg. "There's a big hole and . . ."

"And you'll flip in a second, if you're not careful," interrupted Tuck.

"Hey," said Meg, smiling and poking Tuck's shoulder. "Who's telling this story?"

"Sorry," said Tuck. "Just got carried away."

"Anyway," continued Meg, "Right at that point the cliffs pinch in and the river takes an abrupt 90 degree bend to the left. The river is narrow there and the current is incredibly strong and unpredictable."

"Was this guy told all this?" said John.

"Yes, he was," Jim said, "but the key factor is that the lead guide knew the dangers and allowed the rafter—a customer of the Whitewater Rafting Company—to head out on his own with nothing more than a 'Be careful.' In other words, as the leader he really didn't know where the organization, the Whitewater Rafting Company, needed to go."

"So, what happened to the guy?" asked one of the River Rats.

"He made it to the hole," said Jim, "but there his kayak slammed against the cliffs. The guy was somehow thrown out."

"Did he . . . ?" asked a member of the group.

"Drown?" Jim said. "No, he was lucky. But he nearly did. You see, the guide listened to his customer, but in the process didn't really stay true to the original aims of the company. In essence, he created another set of aims—personal, selfish ones. As leader of this company, he not only had to develop and clearly communicate the aims of the system . . . he needed to make sure that the company had the right aims. And it was after that incident that I took over the Whitewater Rafting Company."

"Quite a story," said Jerri.

"Well, I hope it makes a point," said Jim.

"Yeah," said Mary. "Lets us know that what drives your organization is not just what your customers want, but what they want factored in with your vision of what makes it safe."

"And the expertise to carry it out," added John.

"In a nutshell," said Jim. "Those aims . . . they've got to be translated into goals. And you can imagine—having to come into this company after a near tragic incident like that one, and having to follow a leader who had made some serious errors in judgment, I can tell you that refocusing on the purpose of this company was not easy."

"What did you do?" asked Mary.

"I had to get back to some basics," said Jim. "You know, establish my own vision of what we ought to be and then talk with an awful lot of folks—former customers, employees, even folks in the surrounding community. This is a wilderness, but there are environmental groups that have a vested interest up here, and locals who use the river . . . gosh, an awful lot of folks. And then I had to take that information and make some solid decisions about what were valid needs and expectations; and then, with a small, representative group of stakeholders, translate them into some overall goals for the company." Jim glanced around at the party of River Rats. "Now, enough of my soapbox. Let's talk about Artillery Rapids. Meg?"

"Okay," she said. "They are a Class II-III rapid. Really a relatively easy rapid to run, but it is long, with seemingly no beginning or end. I think you'll find it exciting."

Jim, Meg, and Tuck continued the briefing on the rapids for the day, and then gave the order to push off.

The boats coasted lazily down the Middle Fork. Jim, Meg, and Tuck pointed out various landmarks along the way. Bounded on one side by the Boise National Forest and on the other by the Challis National Forest, this portion of the river featured heavily wooded forests and views of mountains of medium height. The group even had a rare sighting of a bob-

Chapter Four: Customer Aims

cat, standing quietly on an overhanging ledge close to the river's edge. After stopping for lunch and a brief rest at Airplane Camp, the group prepared for the afternoon runs.

"Looks like we've got some clouds moving in," said Jim, checking a portable thermometer he kept in a plastic bag. "It'll keep us a mite cool this afternoon. In fact, these 50's might just stay with us for awhile."

"Could be that timing will be right for Sunflower Flat," said Tuck.

"Right," said Jim. "Folks, if it stays cool like it is now, we have a great surprise in store for you later."

The River Rats donned some extra jackets and then shoved off once more into the river.

Sure enough, the cloud cover hung over the rafting party like a gray cotton canopy. At midafternoon, Jim motioned for the boats to pull over as they approached Sunflower Flat.

"What's the big surprise, Jim?" asked Jerri.

"Yeah. What's at Sunflower Flat?" Mary asked.

"Sunflower Flat is just ahead on the right bank," said Jim. "It's a favorite spot for all our groups because of the magnificent hot springs that pool and then flow into the river." Jim paused. "Anybody interested in a natural 'hot tub' experience?"

A chorus of "Yeah's" rose above the rippling waves of the river, and shortly thereafter, the group pulled onto Sunflower Flat. At the top of an embankment above the river, the rafting party discovered a large pool of water. Steam rose from the surface like mist off a warm lake in the cool hours of morning. Mary ventured close. She removed her shoes and socks and stuck a toe in the pool.

"Whew!" she shouted. "This is hot."

Soon, all the River Rats were soaking in the mineral-rich natural hot springs of Sunflower Flat, resting backs and muscles, sore from hours of paddling.

"Ahh," sighed Jim, who had eased in next to John, Mary,

and Jerri. "This meets my needs . . .how about you guys?"

After the brief but welcome respite, the party regrouped and hit the river again for their last push toward Little Soldiers Camp, their campsite for the night. And just as the sun began to slip behind the tips of the mountains in Boise National Forest, Jim gave the signal to pull into shore. Little Soldiers Camp was located on a small beach just below the river following an unnamed rapid past a left bend in the river. The fire and utility area for the camp was set up next to the river, while areas for the campers' tents were located on the second bench above the fire. This particular campsite was vastly different from previous ones. It was more heavily wooded amidst undulating mounds, which made for interesting sites for pitching tents.

After dinner and time for rest and relaxation, Jim, John, Jerri, and Mary climbed a hillock above the campsite and sat down on a series of natural benches created from fallen trees.

"What an incredible view," said Mary, as she surveyed the bend in the river below, the soothing flames from the campfire, and the shadowy trees, rocks, and outcroppings in every direction.

"John," said Jim, "how about pulling out that list of yours, again?"

John reached into his pocket. The next term on the list following **Leadership** was **Customer Aims**.

"CommonSense.com talked about customers," John remembered.

"You're right," said Jerri. "Internal and external ones. All with expectations."

"Ah," said Jim, "the knowing of who your customers are—and understanding that they have expectations and needs—is your absolute critical first step."

"Just like you knew us," said Mary.

"Mary's right, Jim," John said. "You, Meg, and Tuck

talked with us about our needs. And you listened to us."

"Well," Jim told them. "How else would we be able to determine your requirements and expectations?"

"You wouldn't," said Jerri. "You'd just be guessing and going on personal opinion."

"Be sort of ineffective in the relationship-building game wouldn't it?" said Jim.

"When you put it that way," said John, "it's kind of a no-brainer."

"Remember when I asked each of you to name one thing you wanted to experience on this journey down the river?" asked Jim.

"You mean when we said things like, 'Make it back safe and sound?'" said Mary.

"Right," Jim answered. "Think back to everything that was said and see if you can come up with how I might have translated those needs into aims or purposes, for lack of a better word, for this rafting experience."

"I know one," said Mary. "Safe rafting. Folks want to get back safe and sound."

"Some of the group wanted to make new friends, learn how to work together to guide the raft . . . that sort of thing," said John. "I'd say team building—you know, partnership development, working together as partners in the raft . . . Yes, teamwork, that'd be one."

"Well, folks wanted to fish, go hiking, that sort of thing, too" said Jerri. "That would lead me to say that another one could be a respect for individuality. You know, tied to each person's personal enjoyment."

"I know one more," Mary threw in. "It really has to do with just being able to spend quality time with everyone and with everything we do."

"You hit dead on," Jim said as he stood up and stretched. "Reckon any of that 'knowing your customers and their needs' perspective applies to your school situations?"

And with that, Jim smiled at the three friends and left them sitting together.

"John, do you think your staff feels listened to?" asked Jerri, as she re-positioned herself on the large log. "And as though they are really a part of setting the direction for your school?"

"Good question," John answered thoughtfully. "After what I just heard, I've got a feeling it's something I should work at and not just assume. I mean, I have staff meetings, but I'm afraid I spend most of the time doing all of the talking."

"Saying and spraying," said Mary.

"Yeah," said John, laughing. "I guess that says it all."

"Sounds like your place isn't much different, Mary," said Jerri.

"Don't get me wrong," said Mary. "We have committees and teams . . . but sometimes I think they are more for show than they are truly functioning groups."

"How about you, Jerri?" said John. "Do you do a lot of . . .?"

"Saying and spraying?" interrupted Jerri, smiling and hanging her head. "Guilty. And I have a feeling my folks probably think that it doesn't matter what they contribute because I'm going to do what I want, no matter what."

"Walking the talking," said Mary. "Maybe that should be our new credo instead of saying and spraying."

All three rose from their log seats and made their way back down to camp and a good night's sleep.

Chapter Four: Customer Aims

To Think About – Aims

It is leadership's responsibility to help set the direction for any organization. The way to help set that direction is by listening to the voice of the customer. Leadership talks with and listens to the voice of the customer and determines the AIMS/Purposes of the organization . . . the strategic priorities or customer needs and wants. And in order to truly determine valid aims, leaders must apply two filters: (1) Expertise (2) The Leader's vision of the future.

- ❑ How do you determine customer satisfaction and support?

- ❑ Have you determined who your customers are?

- ❑ How do you enhance relationships with internal and external customers?

- ❑ How do you want to build positive relationships with customers?

- ❑ What methods do you use to listen, learn, and adjust to meet customer requirements?

CommonSense.com

FIVE: Goals and Measures
Aligned Management System

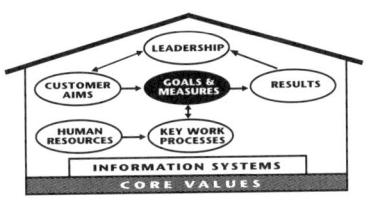

After two days of rafting, hiking, and camping, day three began at a very leisurely pace. The River Rats, despite the soothing waters of Sunflower Flats, woke up sore. Their leaders, recognizing the physical and mental limitations of the group, based on years of experience with hundreds of rafters, decided that going slow and easy would be the rule of the day.

Jerri, John, and Mary woke up early in spite of the sore muscles. They eased out of their sleeping bags and made their way to the campfire, where the smell of coffee cooking over an open fire permeated the brisk morning air.

"Well, good morning," said Jim, who was already sitting by the fire, sipping a cup of the hot, brown liquid. "Muscles a bit tight, I see."

"You're telling me," said John, stretching his arms over his head and arching his back. "I could use another dip at Sunflower."

"Couldn't we all," Jerri said.

"It would meet one of my needs . . . uh . . . aims," said Mary, smiling and rubbing her lower back.

"I think you'll appreciate today," said Jim. "We'll run some rapids, but they won't be the most intense ones, and we'll have some extra time to relax toward the end of the day. We'll get to our campsite a bit earlier than the first two days."

"Sounds great," said John.

The rustle of tent flaps and zizz of zippers signaled the arrival of more of the group, and soon all were sitting together and eating a hearty breakfast.

"All right, River Rats," announced Jim, as breakfast came to an end, "before we head off onto the river for today's adventure, let's recap a bit. Meg, Tuck, and I want to make sure that we are meeting your needs. In other words, that the goals we have set are truly indicative of what you want to do and experience—remembering always that everything we do must be safe and within our expertise to provide. Meg?"

"Thanks, Jim," said Meg. "All right, you guys. I'll sort of go over the areas we've identified that you shared were crucial for a successful experience. Help me out if I get stuck, will you, Tuck?"

"Sure."

"First, Safe and Controlled rafting," said Meg. "Second, Teamwork. Third . . . uh . . ."

"Fun," said Tuck. "Respecting what for you, individually, will bring enjoyment."

"Thanks, Tuck," said Meg. "And fourth, Quality Time—for everything we do."

"Thanks, guys," said Jim. "Now, all of you have some goals—goals tied to wanting to have some fun, to being a team, to enjoying what you do, and to wanting this time—time you paid for, I might add—to be of the highest quality. And John, I believe you said you wanted to be successful at something you'd never done, before. Right?"

"Right," said John.

"Being successful is something we want for all of you, whether the 'having fun' part or the 'I made it back safe' part. So everything you want to do is tied to what drives this orga-

Chapter Five: Goals and Measures

nization. Now, how are we going to know if you're having fun and feeling safe? You know, how are we going to measure that? And you do agree that we ought to measure that, don't you?"

"Well," said Jerri, "the way you put it, if the goal doesn't have a measure of some sort, you won't know whether we liked what we paid for. You might schedule something again that nobody liked . . . or succeeded at."

"Good point," Jim said.

"We'll tell you," said one of the River Rats.

"Well, that's a big part of it," said Jim. "We'll certainly provide some follow-up questionnaires, we'll stop for periodic briefings, and being that you're a pretty 'upfront' kind of group, I don't think you'll have any trouble giving me a piece of your mind most any time. Right?" The River Rats laughed. "But I want to know, as well, how you'll know if you've achieved your goals? In other words, how you're going to measure whether or not it's a 'happening thing' for you?"

"How often I get to stop and fish," said one of the group.

"If we continue to have some leisurely floats along the river as well as the rapid runs," said another. "You know, to give us time to enjoy the sights."

"If we schedule stops at some good hiking sites," said another.

"Hey, I don't want to just fish," said another group member, "I want some results."

"Down the river a bit," said Tuck, stretching out his arm, "there are supposed to be some trout as long as this."

"Just getting my line wet will be enough result for me," said another.

"All right," Jim said, "sounds reasonable. Results—different for everybody, but results just the same. And as we go, we'll keep a check on how we're doing, to make sure we make progress toward those goals. Sound good?"

"Yeah!" the River Rats sounded in unison.

Riding the Wave

The debriefing concluded with a detailed description of the first of the upcoming rapids. The River Rats left the circle on the beach to gather life jackets and do last minute checks.

The three rafts meandered down the river at a leisurely pace. Since, as Jim had promised, there were no rapids of major significance, the trip was a literal experience of the senses of smell and vision. The topography of the land began to change dramatically. Timbered mountains evolved to deep craggy rock faces and semi-arid, rolling hills. Trees were still present, but it was obvious the river's path was taking the rafters into new physical surroundings.

Passing Cameron Creek Camp and Mahoney Camp, the group came upon Whitey Cox Campsite. As they approached the site on the right side of the river, Jim signaled for all the boats to pull onto the sandbar a few paces from the elevated campsite. Soon, they saw shallow pools of water throughout the area. They also saw fish. Fish the length of a man's arm. Swimming lazily around in smooth circles.

"We are camping here, tonight," said Jim. "Some of you wanted to fish, and this is the place. If you can't catch 'em here, then . . ."

"You can't catch 'em," said Tuck, laughing and finishing Jim's challenge.

Meg directed the group to the set-up area on a plateau fifty feet above the river's edge. Upstream was another hot spring on the left side and a single ponderosa pine towering over the area and dominating everything around it.

The River Rats began to set up their tents on the second bench area near the river.

"Hey, look, everybody!" one of the group shouted. "There's a grave marker over here."

"That's Whitey Cox himself," said Meg. "The namesake for this campsite. He was a miner who died in a rockslide while he was prospecting in this area. You can see the date

Chapter Five: Goals and Measures

there, if you rub it off a bit."

"1954," said the rafter.

"Horrible way to go," said another of the group.

"Yeah, but he's immortalized in a grand place," said Tuck. "When I die, I hope they bury me along the river, too."

"Hear, hear," said several of the rafters.

"All right, you guys," shouted Jim. "You've got the afternoon to yourselves. Fish, explore, hike, sleep, read—do it all to your heart's content. Tomorrow it'll be a different story."

～～～～～～～

Jerri, John, and Mary decided to hike a short distance along the river's edge, alternately walking barefoot in the cool, crisp water and sitting along the bank just talking—sometimes sitting and saying nothing, staring at the incredible beauty around them.

"Know what that 'bottom line high profits' thing Jim talked about in that story made me think of?" John said, absent-mindedly scraping a stick along the sand at the edge of the river.

"What?" said Jerri.

"Test scores," Mary said. "Made you think of how we use test scores, didn't it?"

"Sure did," John replied, laughing.

"Causes us to make some decisions that sometimes don't stay true to what we're really about, don't they?" Jerri said.

"You know," said Mary, "Jim said something else interesting that makes me think of test scores, too."

"What's that?" asked Jerri.

"He said they would be checking as we go," said Mary. "You know, to make sure that what we're doing is getting us what we want."

"I see what you mean," said Jerri. "In my school system,

we place tremendous emphasis on that end-of-the-year measure. It's a result that's important, I know, but I sometimes think we get so preoccupied with what that particular result is going to be that we forget the important stuff that leads up to that result."

"Same here," said John.

"Ditto," added Mary.

"Got a feeling that listening better—over time—might make a difference in how we make decisions," said John.

"I'm pretty sure I'm going to be a better whitewater rafter when we're through," said Mary with a smile.

"It's Jim's approach," said Jerri. "Meg and Tuck said it. He talks with—and listens to—his staff and the paying customers. Geez, he even listened to folks in the community."

"And he makes sure our goals have a direct tie . . ."

"Are translated into," interrupted John.

"Huh," said Mary.

"That tie," said John. "It's a translation thing, you know, from the aims. That's how you get your goals and measures."

"I thought his point about measures was excellent," said Jerri.

"Did you notice that they were directly tied to the goals?" said Mary.

"Umm," said Jerri, gazing down the river with its lapping waves, and rubbing her chin. "John, where is that list of terms, again? You know, the ones you copied from the computer screen?"

"Ah," came a voice from behind them. "That famous list, again."

"Whew, Jim," said John. "You scared the daylights out of me."

"Yeah," said Jerri, her hand across her heart, "I thought I was on my way to see Whitey Cox."

"Didn't mean to scare you," said Jim, laughing. "Saw you

Chapter Five: Goals and Measures

guys heading this direction. Thought I'd mosey this way myself."

"We were just talking about school . . . aims, goals, measures," said Mary. "That sort of thing . . . you know, the typical whitewater rafting sort of discussion."

Jim laughed again. "Well," he said, "we might as well jump in. **Goals and Measures**. . . that's next on the list, isn't it?"

"Yep," said John, gazing at the now crumpled but readable paper.

"You know," said Jim, "I figure a big part of my responsibility as leader of this group is to facilitate the establishment and achievement of the goals we set."

"We've written a lot of goals for our school system," Jerri said. "But facilitating the achievement by making sure we actually have measures that tell us something is not something we've done very well."

"Sounds like us," said John. "At my school, we've gotten used to writing goals—or at least what we think are goals—but just haven't developed good, solid measures."

"Ought to happen in the classroom that way, too," said Mary. "Shouldn't it?"

"Remember when I asked whether you thought you ought to measure what you are aiming for?"

"Sure," said John. "I said you'd end up not really knowing whether you were successful or not."

"But how do you know if you have a legitimate measure?" asked Mary.

"Well," said Jim. "First, you need to think about what success would look like if you reached your goal—sort of a definition of success, if you will."

"So what's second?" asked Jerri.

"My rule of thumb," said Jim, touching his outstretched thumb. "No matter how strange a measure may sound, if it gives a picture about your definition of success, then it's a

65

legitimate measure."

"And one measure shouldn't paint the whole picture, should it?" Jerri asked.

"Or pretend that it doesn't . . . but really does," added Mary.

"As far as I'm concerned," said Jim, "in education, results from measures ought to be seen as critical information to help us help children . . . not used as absolute evaluative data that ends up punishing kids for being different." Jim paused. "When we're able to look at goals and measures like that, then we will really begin to change the system of education in this country."

"That's what CommonSense.com is trying to tell us through this Aligned Management System process, isn't it?" said John.

Jim smiled.

"It's beautiful out here, isn't it?" he said.

Chapter Five: *Goals and Measures*

To Think About – Goals and Measures

For every goal, there must be a set of measures to determine if we are making progress on that goal. If the goal can't be measured, then there is no way to determine whether progress is being made. Leadership is responsible for translating aims into goals and measures. This is critical to long-term success of any organization or system.

- ❏ How are internal and external customer needs and wants translated into goals, measures, and action plans?

- ❏ How do you develop goals and measures?

- ❏ How do you determine action plans for deploying and aligning goals?

- ❏ How do you manage goals?

CommonSense.com

SIX: Information Systems
Aligned Management System

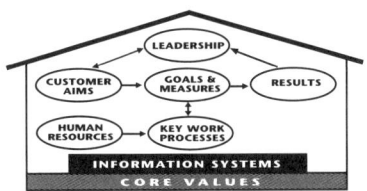

John, Mary, and Jerri stayed up after everyone else had gone to sleep. The campfire continued to burn low, but its warmth was comforting as the three sat together and talked into the wee hours of the night. John's crumpled list of the Aligned Management System terms was the predominant subject for discussion.

"Umm," said John. "Leadership . . . Aims . . . Goals and Measures. Jim's hitting 'em all, isn't he?"

"I'm certainly going to put something in place to help me listen to my parents better," said Mary. "You know, get a feel for their aspirations for their children."

"So you can . . ."

Mary interrupted John ". . . So I can translate those aspirations into classroom goals." She smiled. "I knew you were going to see if I was going to use that 'translate' word. In fact, all this has made me realize I'm the only one in my classroom thinking about goals. If students are going to be leaders, then they ought to develop goals, too."

"As for me," said Jerri, "I'm going to do a better job of gathering input from a lot of groups in my school system. You know, identify some common themes and develop some specific goals around these themes. It would really go a long way toward helping us work better as a team, too."

"And come up with measures, too," said John. "Don't forget that."

"Right," said Jerri. "It's that gathering of data along the way that's tough."

"Ah," said John, as he pointed to his list. "Sounds like 'Information Systems' to me."

"I don't know about you two," said Mary, yawning. "But I think I'm going to sleep on that note."

"Good idea," said Jerri.

"Night, you guys," said John, as he carefully folded the list, placed it in his pocket, and headed for his tent.

All three fell asleep as soon as their heads hit their pillows.

A loud shout broke the early morning quiet in camp.

"Help!" yelled Meg. "We've got trouble!" The shout came from a short distance down the river from the campsite.

The River Rats scrambled from their tents and rushed in the general direction of Meg's voice. As they reached a patch of high sagebrush, they saw Jim, Tuck, and Meg struggling to keep the oar boat containing the food and supplies from drifting further down river.

"Grab on!" shouted Jim. "Somewhere . . . anywhere. We've got to secure this thing!" After a few anxious minutes, the group managed to pull the boat back upstream to the campsite.

"Meg," said Jim, "stay here with me. I want to check and double check this thing again, will you? Tuck, go ahead and get breakfast started." Jim paused and took a deep breath. "Thanks, everybody. Sorry to get you all so wet so early in the morning."

Chapter Six: Information Systems

"Just a simple splash in the face to get us up would have been sufficient," said one of the group, laughing.

"I'll remember that next time," said Jim, forcing a smile, but his displeasure was obvious. Tuck and Meg stood silent.

"How'd it happen?" asked someone. Jim glanced at Tuck and Meg, then took off his hat and wiped his brow.

"The water speed gauge and ranger station guidelines about river depth," said Jim. "I didn't check them like I should have."

"Now, Jim," said Meg. "You . . ."

"No," Jim said, "I had all the information I needed to make sure our boats would stay secure." He paused. "But it just slipped my mind. I thought we were fine for the night . . . but of course, we weren't."

"Coulda happened to any of us," said Tuck.

"Yeah, maybe," said Jim. "But it was something that didn't have to happen." He stood for a moment looking around at all the River Rats. "I guess what I'm saying is that no matter how many times you run the river, and no matter how experienced you might be, don't ever take even one responsibility for granted. Always check and double check the information you have in order to avoid problems."

An awkward silence followed Jim's comments.

"Hey, Tuck," said one of the River Rats, finally breaking the silence. "How 'bout that breakfast?"

"You got it," said Tuck, giving Jim a comforting pat on the back and then heading for the campfire. "Coming right up."

Meg and Jim finished checking the supply boat and then joined the rest of the group, who were already eating.

"What kind of rapids are we running, today?" asked one of the group.

"Well," responded Meg, "we'll start with a fairly easy Class II and then get pretty quickly into progressively more challenging water. You'll get a chance to run several Class III and even some IV rapids today."

"I have a question for Jim," said John.

"Shoot," Jim responded.

"You mentioned something about a water depth gauge, after we brought the supply boat back. And ranger station guidelines."

"Yep," said Jim. "Important information . . . that I didn't use to our advantage last night."

"Well, I was just wondering," said John. "What other information do you . . . uh . . . take into consideration for these trips?" John glanced toward Meg. "I've noticed that Meg scouts ahead sometimes. You and Tuck do, too. Just seemed interesting what kinds of things you guys look for . . . signs . . . you know, that kind of stuff."

"Great question," said Jim. "We've got a number of . . . well, I don't know—guess you could call them information systems—that we consider before, during, and after a trip."

"Weather's one," said Meg.

"She's right," said Jim. "It literally affects everything we do."

"Yeah," Tuck threw in. "If we don't stay in tune with the changing weather conditions we could get ourselves—and you guys—into real trouble."

"Both from a public relations and a safety viewpoint, we constantly collect information on the weather," said Jim. "Remember when I talked about our primary reason for operating as a business? Well, weather affects our ability to meet your aims and needs and to achieve our goals. Could mean a pretty miserable time . . . and it could be dangerous. You guys probably wouldn't recommend us or come back."

"The current in the river would be another one, wouldn't it?" said Mary.

"No question," said Jim. "Current depth, speed—and even the amount of debris that gathers—help us decide which angle

Chapter Six: Information Systems

to attack the rapids as well as how long it will take us to go from one campsite to another." Jim paused. "Even when I talked about collecting data on your attitudes and feelings along the way and after the trip . . . that's really another kind of information system that helps us."

"One other thing," said Tuck. "When I got here, I learned something I hadn't really thought about."

"What was that?" asked one of the River Rats.

"The best information is the information we can actually use."

"Tuck's right," said Meg. "We had to learn what was useful and what wasn't. What wasn't, we didn't collect anymore."

"Remember," Jim told them, "all these information systems are designed to help us make sure the trip is successful. And a successful trip is one that meets all our needs. Collecting this kind of data is critical to long-term success and the welfare of you guys as well as my two cohorts here."

"Sounds like a commercial doesn't he?" said Meg, laughing.

"Why, he could be on TV," said Tuck, mimicking a southern drawl.

"Well," said Jim, his cheeks turning red from embarrassment, "it keeps us getting better and improving all the time." Jim glanced at Tuck. "At least I can speak for some of us." Everyone laughed.

"Hey, let's clean up this place so we can hit the river," said Tuck.

The River Rats finished cleanup in short order. An air of anticipation permeated the group. They had learned some new skills, had been successful, and were ready to try out their newly found confidence on a new section of river. After one more review of the upcoming challenges, Jim, Meg, and Tuck directed the group into their rafts, and the River Rats shoved off for another day's adventure.

After a short time, the group found themselves in Ouzel

Riding the Wave

Rapids, a Class II rapid. It is considered an easy rock garden with a long stretch of rapids churning from rocks just below the surface. Running it was an opportunity for the rafters to refine their paddling skills and prepare them for the remaining higher-class rapids they would run later.

Throughout that day, the rafters bounced, bobbed, lifted, lurched, rubbed, roared, rushed, pushed, dipped, sliced, slid, swished, and splashed their way through narrow openings, over barely submerged boulders, down harrowing drops, and around sharp bends. And by the end of the day, the campsite at Otter Creek was a welcome sight.

After a supper that all devoured ravenously, John, Mary, and Jerri, sensing a need to walk off the calories, found the short trail that Tuck had indicated might be a pleasant respite for anyone wishing to take in some of the marvelous foliage in the area.

"If you're lucky, you might even catch a glimpse of an elk, or if you're really lucky . . . a bobcat," said Tuck.

"Just don't go too far," said Meg, "or stay too long. Finding your way back in the dark will not be fun."

"Watch out for bears!" someone shouted.

Mary, Jerri, and John glared unsettled glances at one another.

"You'll be fine," said Jim. "Just stay on the trail."

"That's comforting," said John. "If we really did see one, what should we do?"

"Shout, wave your arms, act crazy," said Jim. "And here, just to make you feel more comfortable, here's a bullhorn. Just turn this on and blast away. Any critter will turn tail and run."

The three, bullhorn tightly in hand, took their leave of the group and melted into the greens and browns of the pristine forest.

They walked in silence for a short while, admiring pines

Chapter Six: Information Systems

that seemed to touch the sky, huge outcroppings of boulders that burst through the forest floor like giant mushrooms, huge fallen trees making way for younger saplings to stretch their tiny limbs toward the sun, and a mottled green and brown landscape from the foliage of hundreds of species of vegetation. They could hear the roar of the river, now a soothing lull in the distance. The near silence was broken once by a scream they knew to be feline. And here and there, an unknown tiny something would scurry through the underbrush.

"You know that **Information Systems** is next on the list, don't you?" said John, reaching in his pocket, pulling out and then unfolding the piece of paper.

Jerri and Mary nodded in agreement.

Jerri said, "I know we have 'information systems' in my district, but I guess I never quite thought of them in the same way that Jim talked about them."

"There's just a lot more to them," said John, "than just using that test score. Remember what we talked about last night?"

"Jim really opened my eyes," said Mary. "Everyday work, and keeping better track of that—I even thought of ways to create some notebooks that my kids can use to keep track of their own progress."

"I believe you've been thinking on us, here," Jerri said with a smile.

"I know I'm going to look at attendance, disciplinary infractions, tardy rates—those kinds of things—in a different way," said John.

"Remember what Tuck said about 'the best information is the information you can actually use'?" Jerri asked. "That remark really hit me. I know we collect all kinds of information, but not all of it we need. I'm sure of that."

"Goes on a shelf somewhere, doesn't it?" said John.

"Happens in your system, too, eh?" said Jerri, smiling.

75

"Ditto for me," Mary said.

"I guess if we want to continuously get better," said Jerri, "we ought to have the right information systems in place. And for me, the right information is the information that tells us if we're reaching our goals."

"Sounds like a winner to m . . ."

"What's that noise?" said Mary, interrupting John and motioning toward a dense thicket about fifty yards ahead of them. All three stopped dead . . . and silent . . . in their tracks.

"I hear it, too," whispered Jerri.

The three watched as the heavy brush up ahead in the path rustled and swished from something . . . something large . . . that appeared to be moving through it. Through it . . . and toward the three hikers.

"Is . . . is it a bear?" whispered Mary.

"I don't know," whispered Jerri. "But I don't think we should hang around to find out. Where's that bullhorn?"

"Got it," whispered John.

In one swift motion, John held up the bullhorn and faced its bell toward the rustling brush. He flicked the siren switch to on and the loud wail pierced the quiet of the forest. John, Mary, and Jerri looked at each other, turned in one motion and ran back down the path.

Chapter Six: Information Systems

To Think About – Information Systems

Information Systems is like a "House of Quality" because it encompasses the other categories within its structure. All other components of the Aligned Management System must have information systems to collect data on progress. It is the data we collect that helps us make data-driven decisions.

- ❏ How do you select, manage, and use data and information?

- ❏ How do you analyze our performance based on data?

- ❏ How do you evaluate and improve information systems?

- ❏ How do you rely more on data-driven decisions and less on opinion-driven decisions?

- ❏ How do you align information systems to be supportive of the goals and measures?

CommonSense.com

SEVEN: Key Work Processes
Aligned Management System

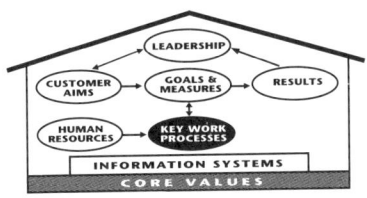

The next morning, Jerri noticed that the guides seemed unusually tense. She mentioned this to John and Mary.

"I figure we'll find out why soon enough," said John.

After the boats were loaded, Jim called the group together for their routine briefing of the day's plans.

"Today will be like no other," he said, "because you're going to experience the river at its most treacherous. Make no mistake . . . this is going to be a tough day."

"We are going to run a series of rapids, one after another," said Meg. "You will be tired and just plain worn out."

"And that's our concern," added Tuck. "You will get so tired that you'll have difficulty being safe."

The River Rats glanced anxiously at one another.

"Lay it on us," said one of the group. "Tell us the bad news."

"Well, for starters," said Jim, "we are going to cover twenty-six miles of the river in one day. Secondly, we are going to run eight different rapids, most of which are Class III or IV."

"I know we've gotten pretty good," said John, "but are we good enough to tackle that challenge?"

"Yeah," said another member of the group. "And is there any good news?"

Riding the Wave

Jim stood up and removed his hat. The few wisps of hair still clinging to his head were already soaked from perspiration from the morning's preparation exertions. He wiped his brow with the large red bandana from his back pocket. A big smile broke across his tanned face.

"We set up this day not to scare you," he said, "but to instill a seriousness about the tasks ahead. This is a day that will challenge your very core—your ability to be in touch with your confidence level, which should be high right now, and your willingness to push yourself to new limits is key. Meg, tell them what the good news is."

"The good news," said Meg, "is that you will make it, and you will be the better for it."

"Now," Jim said, "John, you asked if you folks were skilled enough. Well, we've put a lot of things in place, a lot of key work processes that are designed to help make you—all of us—successful. And these are the things we've done all day, everyday, on this trip."

"We've taught you how to use your paddles," said Meg, "and in a number of different situations. You've had an awful lot of practice."

"All of you know how to secure those safety vests," said Tuck. "They've almost become like a second skin out there, haven't they?"

Everyone nodded.

"We always scout ahead," said Jim, "and as you may remember, Meg has had the most experience in how to scout a river, and for that reason she had the responsibility to set up all our scouting processes. She's the one who taught both Tuck and me, and let me tell you, she's the best around. And, based on our scouting information, we have constantly debriefed and reviewed every set of rapids we've run, and all those things are targeted to help keep you what?"

"Safe," said Mary.

Chapter Seven: Key Work Processes

"It's that knowledge that we believe will help you overcome the tiredness," Jim told them. "And keep safety foremost. Because if we're safe, we'll be successful, and then we'll have..."

"Fun?" said John, interrupting.

"Right on," said Tuck, patting John on the back.

Everyone laughed. It was a nervous laugh, but laughter just the same.

"All right, everybody," said Jim. "Let's go out there and have some fun."

The River Rats pushed the boats from shore. They were quickly caught in the power of the current and moved rapidly along the flow of the Middle Fork. The brief time it took them to reach the first of the eight rapids was paddled in silence. It gave them long enough to marvel at the juxtaposition of the awe-inspiring natural splendor of the countryside against the knowledge of the dangers hidden within the swirling foam and jagged stone. As they always did upon the approach to any rapid, or series of rapids, the River Rats pulled over for a final briefing and preparation. Life vests were checked one more time. Helmet straps were secured and double-checked.

"Well, it's time to get serious," Jim said, "because we are going to begin with the Tappan set of rapids." Then Jim, with Meg and Tuck's assistance, discussed, described, and detailed the information about the upcoming series and the actions necessary to run them safely.

"Just keep your wits about you," said Jim, while directing the rafters to shove off from shore, once more. "And pay attention."

Within a few short minutes, the rafters could hear—and then finally see—the first of the upcoming Tappans. The river ahead was a swirling dervish of water, rocks, limbs, and outcroppings. The river's roar was deafening. Mary, John, and Jerri glanced at one another and managed three anxious thumbs up.

Then, for the next twenty-five miles the River Rats shot

Riding the Wave

rapids, rested when they could, waited on scouting reports, debriefed and briefed, until finally, the last run was completed—the run through Aparejo Point Rapids. The last, to the delight of the River Rats, was the easiest. But—just as Meg had promised—the group had made it, with no more than two broken paddles and a host of sore arms and backs.

"Don't you feel the better for it?" announced Tuck, to the group, as he tied off his boat after they had stopped at the evening's campsite. Tuck's answer was a drenching from a flurry of splashes by the exhausted rafters.

After a meal which some were too tired to eat, all slept well that night. They were awakened later than usual.

"After yesterday," Jim said during breakfast, "you all deserve another day away from any rapids."

"Yes," said Meg, "we've set aside this day as another one to hike, fish, read, write—anything you want to do. Sleep some more if you want."

"For those that want to do some hiking," Tuck told them, "we're at the best place in the world."

"Tuck's right," said Jim, pointing towards the north. "That's Little Pine Mountain over there, and the views from the top are spectacular."

"Some of the best in the west," added Tuck.

"It'll be a real test of your hiking abilities," Jim warned, "because it's a 1400-foot climb up the face of the mountain."

"But it's really worth the climb," Meg said.

"Meg and Tuck will stay here at the campsite area," said Jim, "and help those of you who want to hang around down here. You know, fish, do some less strenuous hiking, that sort of thing. I'll take a group up Little Pine. Who wants to go with me?"

Mary, Jerri, and John chose the climb up Little Pine Mountain, along with several other rafters.

"What kind of . . . uh . . . hiking rating does it have?" said a member of the Little Pine Mountain group. "Easy, moderate, or extreme?"

"Well," said Jim, " a little bit of all three. Starts off easy, then moderate kicks in at some spots, with some easy places here and there. And then the closer we get to the top, the more extreme the hike becomes. It will take us the greater part of the day," he cautioned.

So with water bottles filled, sunscreen applied, hats donned, and hiking boots tied, the group started off.

The first part of the climb was fairly easy. The path meandered gently up the rolling terrain. As the hikers continued to climb, the trail grew steeper and they constantly confronted sharp-angled switchbacks. Soon the rolling hills made way for heavily wooded forest. As the trail steepened, the hikers found themselves spread out along the path. Those with more hiking experience took the lead.

Mary, John, and Jerri moved with the less experienced group; having to stop often to catch a breath became an every few minutes occurrence. Soon, hikers began to drop out and head back down to an easier day around the campsite.

"Whew," said Jerri, leaning over with her hands on her knees, "you guys game for going on . . . or stopping?"

Neither John nor Mary had a quick answer. They were both too out of breath to speak at the moment.

Jim, who had been monitoring the group, walked back to the three.

"Let's rest here for a bit," he said. "Catch your breath. Rest those calf muscles."

John, Mary, and Jerri plopped on the ground on some soft leaves beside the path.

Jim asked them, "Remember, it's that 'not trying' idea that

keeps you from getting to where you want to go."

"The Garth Brooks song," said Mary, still taking in large gulps of air.

"Thought that was just about the river," said John, chuckling through winded gasps.

"Rivers . . . mountains . . . whatever," said Jim. "In the summers, this place is my work, and I think that my team and I do a lot of things here, day in and day out, that truly make a difference for a lot of folks . . . a lot of folks who count on us." Jim pulled out his bandanna to wipe the sweat from his neck. "And it gets pretty tough, sometimes . . ."

"And if you gave up on us," said Jerri, interrupting, "when the going got tough . . ."

"You'd have paid for something you didn't get," said Jim, completing Jerri's thought.

"You say the view is really spectacular?" said John, still wheezing, but beginning to breathe easier.

"There's no view like it . . . anywhere," said Jim. "The ultimate reward."

"Is there a bus at the top?" Mary asked.

Jim laughed. "Look," he said, "Let me share something else with you. Three weeks ago, one of our hikers, Sarah, had back surgery."

"Good grief," said Jerri, incredulous. "She's in that group that's gone on ahead."

"She sure is," said Jim. "And she has no plans to quit this hike no matter how tough it gets or how much pain she has to endure." Jim paused. "Prior to the trip, Sarah let me know about her surgery. When I shared my concerns, she explained why she wanted to come."

"What was her answer?" asked John.

"She said—and I remember it verbatim, 'All that we do in life is a battle with ourselves . . . a battle with our minds. It takes constant self-talk and sheer willpower to set a goal and

Chapter Seven: Key Work Processes

do what it takes to meet that goal.'" Jim watched as the three educators sat together in silence by the side of the trail.

"How about a hand there, Jim?" asked John, breaking the silence and stretching his hand outward. "Guess we won't ever reach the top sitting around here just thinking it's going to get done, now will we?"

Jim pulled John to his feet. John reached out and helped Jerri up. Jerri held out a hand and pulled Mary up. And then the four hikers continued their trek up the side of Little Pine Mountain.

As they neared the summit, they met some of the hikers who had gone on ahead, beginning their return hike.

"Incredible," said one of the group, as he passed John, Jerri, Mary, and Jim. "You were right, Jim. It's breathtaking."

"Sarah's still up there," another said. "She wanted to stay just a bit longer—you know, to take it all in one more time."

When the four finally made the top, they saw Sarah standing by a large boulder, a spot that seemed to open out into a grand panoramic view of the surrounding hills, mountains, valleys, and forests. John, Mary, and Jerri watched as Jim walked over beside her. When she turned, her eyes were filled with tears. Jim put his arm around her shoulders and pulled her to him.

"I'm going to walk on back with Sarah," Jim said as they approached Mary, Jerri, and John, who still stood quietly. "You guys take your time, enjoy the view and your accomplishment today." Jim paused. "Oh, John, have your got your list with you?"

John reached into his vest pocket and pulled out the folded sheet with the list of components from the Aligned Management System on it.

"Hasn't left my side," said John.

"The next component on the list is **Key Work Processes**, isn't it?" said Jim.

"You're right," said Jerri, looking over John's shoulder. "Key Work Processes."

"Sarah reached down deep to get up here," said Jim, patting Sarah on the back. "But she had something else going for her, too."

"She was prepared, wasn't she?" said Mary, smiling at Sarah.

"Ah," said Jim. "The essence of what key work processes do for you." Jim paused. "Prior to coming here, Sarah established her goal and then set about to concentrate on the things she could do every day that would help her reach that goal."

"I . . . I guess you're right, Jim," said Sarah. "I really made my daily routines count—you know, tying what I did to making it to the top of this mountain." Sarah paused. "Gosh, what I ate, how I exercised and rehabilitated my back, making sure that I had just the right kind of shoes . . ."

Chapter Seven: Key Work Processes

"All that stuff," said Jim, interrupting, "All that was the 'stuff' Sarah did, and it wasn't someone else who decided what that stuff was. It was Sarah. She was the one with the hurt back . . . she knew her limitations . . . she knew when she needed to consult her doctor . . ." Jim paused. "But remember, Sarah's goal was not to eat better. It wasn't to exercise more. It wasn't to make her back better. Her goal was to climb this mountain. Doing all that other 'stuff'—preparing, like Mary said—that just helped her to accomplish her goal."

Jim put his arm around Sarah and winked at the three educators.

"See you back at camp," he said.

"You were our inspiration, Sarah," said Jerri.

"You're the woman," said Mary.

John just stood and smiled. "Amazing," he whispered to himself. "Amazing."

As soon as Jim and Sarah had disappeared down the trail, Mary, John, and Jerri walked over to the boulder where they had seen Sarah standing earlier.

"A little more delightful, 'taking of your breath away,' than the climb up, isn't it?" said John.

Jerri said, "It's amazing to me that we're not up here because we rode in some grand helicopter to get here . . . or got some tooshy ride in a comfy SUV."

"What do you mean?" asked John.

"I mean, it was like Jim said about our river trip today, and especially what he said about Sarah," Jerri explained. "You know, the little things we've done every day. Everything we've done to help us come down that river helped us get up this mountain, too. Add some of Sarah's willpower and a little bit of inner conversation . . . and we made this goal."

"Think maybe it has something to do with that alignment CommonSense.com talked about?" said John.

"You're right," Mary said. "All that we've done was designed to help us accomplish what we set out to accomplish."

"I don't think I've ever thought this way about what our school system does," said Jerri. "You know what I mean? Day in and day out?"

"You mean aligning everything to the school system's goals?" Mary asked.

"Now that you think about it," said John, "we've got programs and practices that I'm not sure I could justify . . . or really tell you what they actually help us do."

"Sometimes," said Jerri, "it seems that the stuff we do gets elevated to goal status, and we get bogged down thinking that just implementing that one thing will change everything."

"The old 'silver bullet' theory, eh?" said John.

"Right," said Mary. "Instead of concentrating on the goal of maximizing reading success, I've convinced myself that if I just had this program or that program it would make the difference."

"The key," said Jerri, "is to make sure that the programs help us to achieve our goals."

"Yeah," said John. "Sounds revolutionary, doesn't it? But it's really only . . ."

"Common sense," said both Mary and Jerri, interrupting John. All three laughed.

"There's something else that's got me to thinking," said Jerri.

"What's that?" Mary asked.

"Remember when Jim said Meg was the one who set up the procedures for scouting ahead along the river? And when he said Sarah knew what she needed to do?"

"Yeah," said John. "It was because Meg was the most experienced at scouting . . . the one closest to knowing all about it, I guess."

"And that Sarah knew her own body, and her own limitations," added Mary.

Chapter Seven: Key Work Processes

"Right," said Jerri.

"I know what you're getting at," said Mary. "And it's something that's always been a bone of contention for teachers—namely, we ought to be making an awful lot of the decisions about the programs and strategies that are implemented for our kids."

"You are the closest ones to the day-to-day work . . . you know, of actually teaching," said John.

"But don't forget about that alignment issue," Jerri said. "If the workers closest to the work don't make sure that the key work processes are in alignment with the goals . . . well . . . "

"Makes me think back to those many discussions we had about core values," said John.

"Yes, you're right," said Mary. "Let's see, employee participation . . . partnership development . . . "

Jerri interrupted. "It'll mean greater buy-in from everybody if everybody has a part."

"And higher performance," said John.

The three stood and gazed out over the rolling green below them. Far below, they could see the river meandering through the valley.

"You guys ready to head back?" asked Jerri.

"Let's stay just a bit longer," said Mary.

Riding the Wave

Chapter Seven: Key Work Processes

To Think About – Key Work Processes

Key Work Processes are the methods or "things we do" to accomplish the goals we want to accomplish. They are the programs, services, and strategies that are designed, implemented, and improved. It is crucial that the workers closest to the work to be done have a significant say in the determination of the programs and strategies to be implemented.

- ❏ How do you design processes, programs, services, and strategies in alignment to our goals?

- ❏ How do you manage processes, programs, services, and strategies?

- ❏ How do you continually improve core processes?

- ❏ How do you work with partners to improve these processes?

- ❏ How do you align daily activities to goals?

CommonSense.com

EIGHT: Human Resources
Aligned Management System

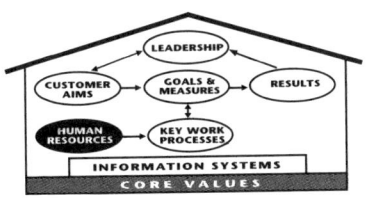

Before Jerri, John, and Mary even reached camp, the tantalizing aroma of plank roasted salmon and cornbread pudding greeted them along the return trail from the top of Little Pine Mountain.

"Tuck's at it again," Mary said.

"He can cook at my house any day," said John, taking in another long whiff of the sweet fragrance from the cornbread skillet.

"Wonder if he hires out?" Jerri mused as she anticipated those tender salmon flakes soon to be melting in her mouth.

The three educator friends made the last fifty yards down the Little Pine Mountain trail to camp in record time. The long and tiring trip to the top . . . forgotten.

"Tuck, my man," said John, "you are one great chef."

"I resemble that remark," said Tuck, laughing, then adding, "Thank you . . . it's a pleasure cooking for you guys."

"Tuck couldn't even boil water before he joined us," Jim said, winking at Tuck.

"You're kidding," said Jerri. "Why . . . he's a pro."

"Yeah," said Mary. "I would've sworn he'd been cooking all his life."

"Jim sent him to 'cooking school,'" Meg said.

"Well," said Jim, "as the leader of this motley crew, I knew that meals were a big deal with rafters—and food poisoning doesn't bring people back. Know what I mean?" Jim snitched a taste of cornbread pudding. "So, if we were going to meet our aim for a successful and safe experience—and since one of our goals to accomplish that was to serve quality meals—I knew that one of us needed training in how to do it right."

"Jim picked me," said Tuck, patting his belly, "because I like to eat so much."

"Well, the result for me has been total satisfaction," said Jerri, patting her own belly.

"Mealtime by Tuck," said John, winking at Jim. "A real 'information' system designed to get delicious results."

"All *right*," exclaimed Jim, opening his eyes wide and giving John a big thumbs up.

"Sounds like commonsense, to me," said one of the other members of the group.

John, Mary, and Jerri immediately looked at each other, then in one motion turned toward Jim.

Jim just smiled.

The meal that evening, as all had expected, was a culinary delight. The River Rats ate against the backdrop of a sky clear and full of stars. The constant, rhythmic burble of the river was their quiet, dinner music. Conversation was light. The rafters sat in small groups on cut log benches or paired off around the fire, squatting on the ground, leaning against tree stumps.

While forking another bite of salmon, John looked casually across at two members of the group eating and talking together. One must have told the other a joke because there was a loud laugh. As John watched and wished he had been in on the joke, he suddenly saw the laugher stop mid-laugh and grab for his throat. But before John even realized that the

Chapter Eight: Human Resources

man was choking, he saw Jim, Meg, and Tuck appear as if out of nowhere. Meg and Tuck pulled the young man to his feet, while Jim circled to his back, encircling the man's waist with his arms. In one quick jolt, Jim squeezed. A small morsel of food popped out of the man's mouth and landed at the feet of his astonished friend.

For an instant, everyone sat as if frozen. Then two hands began to clap. Gradually, everyone joined in a rousing ovation for Jim, Meg, and Tuck. The young man, now a bit sheepish, shook each rafting team member's hand.

"Swallow first . . . then laugh," said Jim, smiling and patting the young man on the back.

"That's about the quickest Heimlich maneuver response I've ever seen," said Jerri, walking over to the three leaders of their rafting adventure. John and Mary followed.

"It was almost like you knew he was going to choke before he did," said John. "I even saw him when it happened. But even so, my brain couldn't get the message to my feet to get up to do anything—much less remember how to do the Heimlich."

"We've got to be prepared for a lot of things," said Jim. "We train ourselves for just about any occurrence. Helps us to anticipate problems . . . sometimes stop them before they happen."

"But you worked together as an amazing team, too," said Jerri.

"Yeah," Mary said. "That's sort of been obvious all along —you know, the respect you have for one another . . . how much you depend on each other."

"Well," said Jim, putting his arms around Meg and Tuck, "I figure my team members are about the greatest resources I've got. Making sure they get the training they need to feel successful helps to make you guys—our customers—successful."

"He's right," Meg said. "The better I'm prepared for what's

in store, the more confidence I have. The more confidence I have that I can handle and face the trip, the more likely I . . . we . . . will be successful." Meg paused. "I know Tuck feels the same way. And I've got to hand it to Jim. As our leader, he's the one who helped us to realize this . . . and made sure that we got the training we needed."

"That's why we've been successful rafters, too, isn't it?" said Jerri, nodding her head and smiling as she looked at John and Mary. "It's something you've been alluding to all along, and I think . . . for the first time . . . it has just sunk in." Jerri paused. "We were prepared, because of your expertise, even for the scary stuff, so we knew what to do when the time came."

"Makes sense to me," said John.

"You mean, commonsense, don't you?" said Mary, laughing.

"Well," said Jim, "the well-being of my team is crucial. They really have to be more than just well-prepared technically. They have to be well-prepared mentally and emotionally."

"And Jim is great at that," said Meg. "It's not enough to just know that I have the knowledge to do something. It's important that I know that Jim knows that I do, and that he has confidence in me."

"We trust each other," said Tuck, "and we look after one another, too."

"Speaking of looking after one another," Jim said, speaking to everyone, "tomorrow is our last day and . . . " There were groans from everyone. "Now, now, I thought I'd at least hear a cheer or two . . . well, as I was saying, tomorrow is our last day on the river. It will be a short one. We'll pull into Cache Bar, our take-out point. Your assignment: I want you all to be prepared to share one experience during our Awards Luncheon. Tuck, Meg, and I will have some special awards to pass out."

"All *right!*" shouted one of the group members.

Chapter Eight: Human Resources

"Hey, you all have worked hard," Jim said, "and you deserve some recognition for what you've done." Jim looked at Meg and Tuck. "It's probably our favorite time during the trip. And one of the most important pieces of our program." He took off his hat and wiped his brow. "Now, let's police this camp . . . and get a good night's sleep."

Jerri, John, and Mary decided to sit up awhile on this last night before they would be traveling home. The fire still glowed from the slowly dying embers, and its warmth was comforting to the three friends . . . three friends who had grown closer during this whitewater rafting adventure. As they watched the soothing flames, they heard quiet footsteps approaching.

"Jim," said Jerri, smiling and poking John in the stomach. "Must be list time."

John, on cue, retrieved the worn sheet once more.

"**Human Resources**," said Mary, reading over John's shoulder.

"It's a biggie for me," said Jim.

"Well, it's really obvious," said Jerri, smiling at Jim. "What you just talked about tonight translates, in our education settings, to employee well-being, recognition, and staff development."

"Couldn't have said it better, myself," said Jim. "I figure if my team . . . or you guys . . . don't have the skills to do what needs to be done to accomplish our goals, we might as well be . . ."

"Just flapping in the water?" Mary interrupted Jim.

"Ah, you remember from that first day, don't you?" said Jim. "You might want to circle Human Resources on that paper. Twice."

With that, Jim tipped his hat and headed for his tent. Jerri, John, and Mary remained by the campfire.

"Pretty impressive today, wasn't it?" said Mary.

"You mean the Heimlich thing Jim did?" asked John.

"Well, that . . . and everything, I guess," said Mary. "I'm kind of like Jerri. Watching the three of them in action and then talking about it sort of helped bring some things together for me."

John was thoughtful. "I don't know that I've always prepared . . . or seen to it that the opportunity for good solid preparation existed . . . for my folks."

"Can you imagine what it would be like if Meg and Tuck and Jim's whitewater rafting skills were only a result of being told that they were supposed to take over this new company one day," said Jerri, "and then had to start taking folks out the next day."

"You mean sort of a . . . Yeah, that's a river and it has whitewater on it, let's go . . . kind of thing?" said John.

"It's what we ask our teachers—our staffs—to do too often," said Jerri.

"I remember a new math program we were told to implement," said Mary. "I believe I received a book after the salesperson gave us her spiel."

"Solution of the month?" said John.

"Well, none of our folks had any real ownership in the concepts or philosophy behind the program," said Mary. "Our only training was the salesperson's pitch . . . and the book."

"You're right," said Jerri, "We've had a tendency to let publishers dictate curriculum and then assumed teachers would just be able to take the books or programs or whatever and on their own . . ."

"Do their thing?" added John.

"Bull's-eye," said Mary. "But what's worse, I would end up blaming the salesperson or the program if no real improvement resulted at the end of the year." She paused. "If I had known what I know now . . . first, I would have made sure my

Chapter Eight: Human Resources

classroom goals and measures were clear . . . and aligned to our school goals. And then I would have figured out which parts of the program or book really helped us to accomplish those goals."

"Incredibly obvious strategies now, aren't they?" said Jerri, shaking her head both in disbelief and relief at the wealth of strategies that were beginning to fill her mind. "You know, I really liked Jim's comments about Meg and Tuck being his best resources."

"Yeah," said John, "the human kind."

"I like that," said Mary. "I like thinking of myself as a resource—an important resource that ought to be trained to do what needs to be done to accomplish the goals."

"And to be treated like a team member whose well-being is important," added John.

"And to be recognized for doing what it takes to get there," said Jerri.

"My students," said Mary with a hint of a smile as if from an inner light bulb, "my students—all this, it applies to them as well. How I prepare them to do what they need to do. How I recognize them for their accomplishments. How I help develop our classroom into a team. It . . . it all fits."

"John," said Jerri, motioning for Mary to come closer, "let's see that Aligned Management System list again."

John held up the list. The wear and tear during the trip had taken its toll, but it was still readable. Mary and Jerri stared at each other for a brief instant.

"Put two circles around 'Human Resources,'" they said, simultaneously. Then they laughed.

Riding the Wave

Chapter Eight: Human Resources

To Think About – Human Resources

The Human Resources component consists of employee well-being, recognition efforts, and staff development. If an organization has legitimate and worthy goals, but the workers don't have the skills necessary to accomplish these goals, then success is likely to be limited at best. Human Resources examines how our systems (and subsystems) enable workers to develop and utilize their full potential, aligned to the goals of the system.

- ❑ How do you ensure teamwork?

- ❑ How do you recognize contributions to improvement?

- ❑ How are workers trained and prepared to 'do the work'?

- ❑ How is the training deployed related to the goals?

- ❑ How do team members regularly comment on their own needs and satisfaction levels?

CommonSense.com

NINE: Results
Aligned Management System

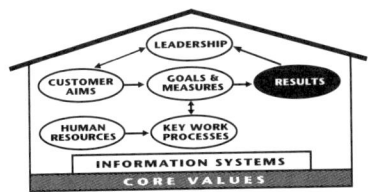

Morning came. And the sunrise found Jim, John, Jerri, and Mary sitting around Tuck's early breakfast campfire. The rest of the camp, except for Meg, who had gone ahead one more time to scout the river up to Cache Bar, still slept. Sparks crackled off the dry wood, and the wafting smoke, coupled with the dark bean perfume of the first pot of coffee, permeated the air around the four as they sat upon the log benches.

"I never get tired of this," said Jim, as he stared at the creeping golden reds of the sun's rays peeking over the mountains and dancing off the tall evergreens, casting the first shadows of a new day.

"Look," Mary said, pointing upward over the trees.

"An eagle," John whispered, watching as the great bird soared high above them. And then almost to himself, he said, "... drifting on the wind."

"A high performance journey is like a river," added Jerri.

"Drifting and paddling along wherever it takes us," said John.

"Learning continuously as we go," finished Mary.

"You guys have really kept yourselves focused on the journey this week, haven't you?" said Jim.

"Well," said John, chuckling softly, "we have gotten to be pretty good rafters."

"I have a feeling," said Jim, "that the 'river' systems you guide back home are going to look a bit different now, don't you think?"

Before any of the three could answer, they heard their River Rat companions stirring. Jim stood up.

"Before you leave the motel in Stanley we'll get together one more time."

After breakfast, Jim called the River Rats together to review what to expect during that last day. Meg had reported nothing unusual on the river ahead. Following the briefing, the group prepared themselves quickly and efficiently.

"I believe you folks are becoming seasoned veterans," said Jim proudly as he entered his raft and readied for push off. But the group did not respond as their usual rowdy selves, and Jim knew why. He could read it in their expressions. From his experience and observations over time, Jim knew that this group of River Rats was not unlike so many that had come before them. They had been successful. They had encountered obstacles . . . and overcome them. He knew that it was not so much the river that they had conquered, but themselves. The river had merely been their vehicle. And the River Rats were both happy and sad at the same time. Happy to have reached their goals. Sad that they were leaving this river. But Jim knew that what they had experienced on this river would help them on any "river" they encountered. He also knew, that for many, that realization wouldn't come until much later. For his three protégés, he believed the realization to be a part of them now.

Chapter Nine: Results

This was the result he had hoped and planned for—a result that wasn't measured by numbers but a solid, valid result, just the same. He would get his numbers later, too. The team always asked their customers to fill out a survey prior to leaving. And they would also keep track of repeat customers—a measure that was extremely important to them. He wanted people to come back. He had learned that if he listened to their needs, set goals to meet them, constantly assessed and measured along the way, taught them what they needed to know to be successful, and made sure his team put the processes in place to make all this happen . . . that the results would speak for themselves.

Jim paused in his thought, then smiled inwardly. It occurred to him that the lessons of the river now permeated every aspect of his life. He had accepted that it was a good and positive thing to strive to improve in everything he did . . . to never be satisfied to the point that he no longer wanted to grow. A richness and fullness existed in his life now that transcended all the 'trials and tribulations' that he, like everyone else, had to face everyday. His thoughts, again, drifted to Mary, Jerri, and John. *It's going to happen for them, too.*

Once on the river, the group soon reached the confluence of the Middle Fork and main stem of the Salmon Rivers. The area was like a wind tunnel and the breezes picked up considerably. With the emergence of the wind and the turbulence created by the joining of the forks, the River Rats were reminded of the power of nature . . . the power of the river system and its elements.

"Keeps you honest, doesn't it!" Jim shouted to the group, over the roar.

"I have erased over-confidence from my vocabulary," John

remarked to Jerri and Mary, paddling beside him.

The group soon passed Stoddard Pack Bridge and Placer Creek. After that, their last rapid, an unnamed Class II+, was a short ride. But it provided a last, magic reminder of the previous days' adventures.

Upon reaching Cache Bar, the River Rats, now just regular people again, unloaded their boats, reorganized their gear, and loaded the waiting truck. All this done, it was time for the Awards Luncheon.

Jim, Meg, and Tuck had secretly decided on special awards for each member of the group. Everyone received an award. One of the group had discovered a piece of a paddle that had broken during their most treacherous day on the river. It had floated down river and lodged in a rock crevice close to shore. She had hidden it until this last day to present to Jim, Meg, and Tuck. The three leaders accepted the "Broken Paddle of Honor Award" for "Leadership, Unwavering Support, Being Great Listeners, Being Prepared, the Masters of the Heimlich, and Just Generally Putting Up with Our Mess."

When it was time for the sharing, each member of the group stood and recounted an experience . . . a thought . . . something . . . that was particularly special to them about the trip. Jerri, John, and Mary went last.

"I learned many lessons while on the river," said John. "And it's uncanny how they apply to my work as a school principal." He paused. "I've got so many that it's hard to choose."

"We're in trouble now!" someone shouted out. "He's going to make a speech."

Everyone laughed, including John.

"I promise to keep it short," he assured them. "One of the things I learned was to listen better. Jim talked so much about listening to us, his customers, and then interpreting our needs and expectations so that he and his team could really develop some sound purposes and aims. I know that as the leader of

Chapter Nine: Results

this company he has a vision about the experience and aims that are an outgrowth of that, and he used his vision to make our aims be valid and true ones." John paused. "I want to do that in my school. I want to establish some processes that will help me listen to my staff better, and that will help my staff and me listen better to our customers—our children and their parents—and all those folks who have a stake in the success of my school." John paused again and looked over at Mary and Jerri, who were smiling. "I've got a list here, in my pocket, that outlines seven components that I know I must attend to if I'm going to see improvement in my school. Like Jim has done with this rafting company . . . he's attended to all of them. What I've just talked about is one of them. And what I guess I've done is to begin to think about creating an action plan for myself to begin 'attending' when I get back." Everyone applauded and John sat down.

"Guess it's my turn," said Jerri, standing up. "You know, just the opportunity to get away, to see another part of the country, was worth everything. To be able to do that, and to grow as an educator at the same time, was almost more than I could have asked . . . but that has happened." She stopped and gave a slight nod to Jim. "I guess I was particularly struck by the importance Jim placed on people during this trip. And the mutual respect that obviously exists within his team. You know, we talk about Human Resources a great deal in education but I'm not sure I truly appreciated what attention to Human Resources really meant until I had to travel down this river. All of us had parts to play this week. All of us had to know our part. But we all had to recognize that our part can't stand alone . . . it must fit together with all the other parts. And we had to feel good about the part we played, and the role it played to make the entire trip a success for everyone . . . in addition to our own individual successes. I've gotten to know some new folks." She looked over at John and Mary.

"And to know some better. And I have been thinking about my own action plan when I get back to my school system, and how I will attend to those seven things John made reference to earlier." Everyone applauded and Jerri sat down.

"Guess I'm last," said Mary.

"But certainly not the least," said Jim, smiling. Mary smiled a thank you and then stood up.

"Well, John and Jerri made reference to that list," said Mary, "and it's a list that has been a revelation for me, too. Aside from thoroughly enjoying the incredible sights and the 'opportunity' to climb Little Pine Mountain . . ." Everyone who had tackled the trail laughed. They knew what a challenge that opportunity had been. "I think what struck me most was how Jim, Meg, and Tuck tied everything we did to helping us have a great time on this trip. And by great time, I mean we were kept safe; we got to do some things on our own; we got to feel successful; we ate some wonderful food . . . I guess I could on and on." Mary stopped and looked again at Jerri and John. "All those things—those day-in and day-out things that Jim, Meg, and Tuck did—really were an eye-opener. As a teacher, I always thought I should just be allowed to go into my room and close my door—you know, just let me teach?" She paused again, taking a deep breath. "But there's more to it than that. Much more. My action plan will begin, too, when I return to my classroom."

And thus, with humor, sincerity, and fondness, the group reflected on their time together. And the evidences of success collected at this final gathering were just as Jim had predicted.

As the group finished the luncheon, Meg announced, "We'll be boarding the bus in thirty minutes."

Jim approached Jerri, John, and Mary, who were still seated at their luncheon table.

"All right, John," said Jim. "One last time, bring out that list."

Chapter Nine: Results

"**Results**," they all said in unison.

"Did you see the natural tie between goals, measures, and results?" he asked.

"Another strong role for leadership, isn't it?" remarked Jerri.

"If I don't take the information that you guys provided and look at it in relation to the data I've gotten before you—and what I'm going to get after you—then I just haven't monitored very well."

"And the decisions you make won't necessarily be very solid, right?" asked John.

"You know," Jim said, "I even have to take into account information from other rafting companies . . . what's happening with them . . . how our experience compares—that kind of thing."

"Sounds like something that really has to happen and show up over a period of time," said Mary.

"Well," Jim said, "if we're going to have any idea of what success looks like, we've got to key in on results."

"But you have to be able to measure them, right?" John asked.

"Absolutely," said Jim. "You know, all these components are connected . . . in a big way. And important—real important—is that leadership must make sure they are connected. This is where your real strategic planning cycle happens. That connecting of the components . . . the listening to customers, then establishing valid aims, deriving aligned goals and measures, and reporting results back to customers on a regular basis. And then doing it over and over . . . over time." Jim paused again. "And it's only over time that progress and real change in your system will begin to happen. Now, fold up that list and frame it when you get back home."

John, Jerri, and Mary laughed and headed for the bus, which would return them to the motel in Stanley. It was a quiet ride back. Except for the heavy breathing of those in the group who snored.

The bus arrived at the motel late that afternoon. Most would spend the night, catching planes the following morning.

Jim approached the three educators. "Meet me in fifteen minutes in the café," he said.

Chapter Nine: Results

To Think About – Results

The Results component examines the performance of the system by establishing baseline performance and performance over time. Leadership looks at results, not only over time, but how these results compare to similar organizations and other world-class organizations. Results tell us what success looks like. They must be measurable. Leadership must monitor and track the organization's progress by assessing results and sharing, with customers, on an ongoing basis how the organization is doing.

- ❑ How do you measure and report results that show how highly customers value your products and services?

- ❑ How do you measure and report performance results?

- ❑ How do you adjust your plans based on what the data tells us?

- ❑ How do you measure and report results that show satisfaction levels?

CommonSense.com

TEN: A Time for Farewells
Aligned Management System

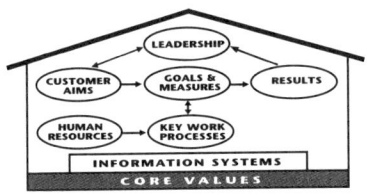

After fifteen minutes, the four gathered around a booth in the small café at the motel.

"Jim," Jerri asked, "why have you done this . . . why have you given so much of your time to help us?"

"Yes," said John, "you've gone out of your way to help us understand the Aligned Management System."

"And you used a river, of all things, to show us," said Mary.

"I need to share with you," said Jim, after pausing to organize his thinking, "that I am a practicing educator in a school system not far from here. I love being a river guide in the summers, but my first love and vocation is teaching. You ask why? I'm concerned . . . concerned about the direction education is going. And I'm concerned about the way we go about finding solutions to our problems."

"I think I know what you mean," said Jerri. "We tinker here, tamper there, try this for a little while, then switch to that. Look for first one silver bullet and then for another."

"There's a disconnectedness about it all, isn't there?" remarked Mary.

"I think Jim would use the term, 'mis-alignment,' wouldn't

you, Jim?" said John.

"We absolutely must improve our schools," said Jim, "if this nation is to survive and prosper—and if our young people are going to be successful in life, work, and in maintaining all that is good about our democratic way of life."

"Just tinkering and tampering doesn't improve the system, does it?" said Jerri.

"Well, it's that new knowledge that is going to make the difference," Jim answered. "The Aligned Management System is not a silver bullet. But it is a framework for—a way of thinking about—continuous improvement and high performance over time. Until educators understand the notion of systems thinking, little improvement is likely to occur. Remember when I stressed the issue of my rafting team's well-being? And Meg talked about being prepared technically, mentally, and emotionally, and knowing that I have confidence in her? Well, I realized how crucial that aspect is for my school . . . and any degree of success it may have . . . and any chance for real improvement and high performance to happen."

"I guess everyone has to be thinking 'system', don't they?" John asked.

"Precisely," said Jim.

"But you still haven't answered why us," said Mary. "Why did you choose us?"

"I didn't choose you," said Jim.

"CommonSense.com," said John. "That's who chose us, right?"

"Well, actually," said Jim, "you chose yourselves."

Mary, Jerri, and John stared blankly at one another.

"There are thousands of educators like us throughout the country," said Jim. "You . . . we . . . all want to do an even better job but often lack the knowledge, confidence, and new skills necessary in today's world. It isn't about being competent, but rather about learning new skills to meet today's needs.

Chapter Ten: A Time for Farewells

And that's where the Aligned Management System comes in. It's the roadmap—the blueprint—to help you . . . us . . . find even greater success in the future."

Jerri, John, and Mary sat in silence. Jim took off his hat and wiped his brow.

"Then who really is CommonSense.com?" asked Mary, finally breaking the silence.

Jim looked first at John, then to Jerri. There was another long pause.

"I . . . I think I finally understand," said Jerri, smiling at Jim.

"Tell them," said Jim.

Jerri turned and looked at John and Mary. "It's us, isn't it, Jim?" she said.

Jim smiled.

"We . . . all of us who want to get better than we are . . . all of us who are truly committed to children and their welfare . . . all of us who know that it will take something different than what we are presently doing to make a change . . . it is the strength of our combined restless spirit of dissatisfaction with the way things are . . . our heart . . . that created CommonSense.com."

"You mean," said John, "that all that new learning has been in us all along?"

"In a sense," Jim explained. "For much of what is on that map—that blueprint—we already know. We just don't know that we know. And just as important, we are afraid to take that leap of faith to make the true change that will make a true difference."

"And we created CommonSense.com to bring it to the surface," said Jerri.

"You mean we've been talking to ourselves all this time?" said Mary.

"That combined strength of commitment . . . and deter-

Riding the Wave

mination," said Jim, "created a powerful new entity that embraced your . . . our . . . will; took what was merely in us all the time and reconfigured it into that new blueprint . . . that new framework."

"And now it's up to us to use it, isn't it?" said John.

"And now," Jim said, "it's time to ride the wave."

Epilogue

The Aligned Management System is based on the seven components found in the Baldrige Performance Excellence Criteria. Our first book, *CommonSense.com*, illustrated the Core Values of this criteria in action and now *Riding the Wave* illustrates the seven components of an interrelated, interconnected system for continuous improvement. Language used in this book is not exact to Baldrige; however, it is intended to speak to the reader in language that begins the learning journey.

Life is a Mystery!

Life is a mystery.
Just when you think you understand your purpose,
Your reason for existence —
A new challenge — a new opportunity — is presented.

Sometimes you want to run and hide
from these new challenges.
Sometimes you want to simply say:
"Leave me alone — let others do it!"

But you realize that avoidance
is not only improbable–
It's impossible.

Educating kids is a mystery.

Just when you think you've found a way
to meet their needs,
A new challenge — a new opportunity — is presented.

Sometimes you want to run and hide
from these new challenges.
Sometimes you want to simply say:
"Let others do it!"

But then you realize that avoidance
is not improbable—
It's impossible.

You realize that avoidance
is a major issue in education—
That taking risks and focusing new challenges
is not for someone else to do.

And especially when so many are counting on us
To Succeed!

-All the Best-

CommonSense.com

NOTES

NOTES

NOTES